Old Dog

Barney Bardsley

SIMON &
SCHUSTER

London · New York · Sydney · Toronto · New Delhi

A CBS COMPANY

First published in Great Britain by Simon & Schuster UK Ltd, 2013
A CBS COMPANY

1 3 5 7 9 10 8 6 4 2

Simon & Schuster UK Ltd
1st Floor
222 Gray's Inn Road
London WC1X 8HB

www.simonandschuster.co.uk

Simon & Schuster Australia, Sydney
Simon & Schuster India, New Delhi

A CIP catalogue record for this book is
available from the British Library

ISBN: 978-1-47110-128-1
Ebook ISBN: 978-1-47110-129-8

Typeset in the UK by M Rules
Printed and bound by CPI Group (UK) Ltd, Croydon, CRO 4YY

Old Dog

Also by Barney Bardsley

A Handful of Earth

Flowers in Hell: An Investigation
into Women and Crime

for my daughter
Molly Rose

Contents

Introduction

I was never really a fan of old dogs – until now. They unnerved me, made me ill at ease. There is something uncanny in the way they fix you with their milky, far-away eyes, more than a whiff of mortality in their creaking joints, their stiff and lumpy frames. When you are young, the truth about ageing is the last thing you want to see and hear – living forever is the only possible option – but I am no longer young and neither is my dog.

She is fifteen years old and getting more fragile with every passing day. She is smelly and eccentric and increasingly random in her behaviour. I hover over her, as a midwife might hover at the arrival of a brand-new baby, yet I know that I am presiding not at a beginning, but an imminent end. Despite all this, or maybe because of it, I do not feel in any way estranged from my ancient pet, altered though she is in character and faculty by her various illnesses and failing strength. I find, to the contrary, that I love her more and more as the strange, precious days of her dotage pass by. She has been with me for twelve years, through good and bad and indifferent. She has stood by me. Now I stand

by her, and I am grateful. For not only has she helped me overcome my youthful fears of frailty and senescence, but she has
also proved, with honour, the early and heartfelt intuition of my
youth: that there is no animal more loving and rewarding to have
in your life at any age than a dog.

It all began when I was seven and asked for a puppy for my
birthday. To my astonishment, my wish came true. A small candidate was chosen from the litter of a local farm dog and, six
weeks later, she came home to us. There she flourished for the
next fourteen years, till she died of simple old age. We named
her Tess. These days, dogs are likely to be called all manner of
fancy things. In my family there has been a recent run on food-
stuffs – a Muffin, a Nutmeg and a Marmite. Further afield, I have
noticed a rap gangster theme, with a dashing Snoop (Doggy
Dog) and a slinky (Slim) Shady in my acquaintance. But when
I was a child, the inspiration was pure Thomas Hardy, so 'Tess'
arrived in our midst.

She was a multicoloured terrier-cross mongrel, with a face
made for mischief and a temperament to match. Before she
came, my mother was adamant about the rules: the dog would
stay in the kitchen most of the time and must learn her place; she
would never be allowed on the furniture and certainly not per-
mitted to eat off our crockery or to take doggy liberties of any
kind. Was that clear? It was quite clear.

The day came for her delivery. The man who owned the
litter marched confidently into the front room with a small,
squirming bundle under his arm. My mother's friend was round

for tea and sat decorously in an armchair, eager to see the new arrival. Before she knew what was happening, the owner deposited the puppy straight onto her lap, saying, 'Oh, she's going to love it here!' At which point, tiny Tess stuck her snout into Mrs Ellis's teacup, took a big slurping drink and promptly piddled all over her well-dressed lap. And that was that – so much for the rules.

This is the way it is with dogs. You think you own them, but they *know* they own you and, one way or another, your meek puppy pet will wreak total havoc, either physically or emotionally, during the course of its canine career. Tess was never really my dog. She distributed herself around the family with careless largesse and boundless enthusiasm. But I loved her dearly, as did we all, even when she drove us mad with her noise, her disobedience and her Houdini-like talent for disappearing: she would turn up hours later, messy and happy, just when the whole family had given her up for dead.

We had other animals too – two cats and a randy white rabbit – but Tess was the best. She fostered in me a lifelong delight in dogs of every shape, shade, personality and size. I can walk by a baby's pram, quite oblivious to the billing and cooing of other adults and the charm of the pram's inhabitant, but show me a dog, tied up outside a shop, waiting sadly for its owner to reappear, and I simply cannot resist. Even if I refrain from a stroke or the offer of a hand to sniff, I always speak a few encouraging words, stand for a second in admiration and make some reverence, human to canine, some small acknowledgement of my respect, before reluctantly moving on.

Despite this almost unseemly devotion to dogs, I was well into my forties before I had one of my own. I'm not quite sure why it took so long. Living in London in a third-floor flat, keeping irregular hours and leading a somewhat chaotic life may have played a part. But marrying and moving to the north of England, with a small child and a seriously ill husband, changed everything. Suddenly there was a house and a garden. Then, in 1999, there was a dog.

The arrival of Muffin, a rescue mongrel, altered all our lives for the better. My life, twelve years on, has remained changed and infinitely improved. Muffin turned out to be a rather wise and weather-beaten little soul, sent not only to be a joyful companion in the usual doggy way – with all those playtimes, toys and bouncy long walks – but also a teacher, a nurse, a silent therapist, as she accompanied me through times of hardship and heightened distress, and participated in the cheerful mundanities of everyday life.

It seems only fitting to write about this dog – and of her transition, quiet and uncomplaining, into extreme old age – if only as a tribute to her unflinching steadfastness. She stands for the millions of other dogs, worldwide, who fulfil – in their loyalty towards humans, who are often so much less than loyal in return – a function that is unique in the animal kingdom. Dogs were custom-built to walk by our sides, and that is exactly what they do.

The idea of the book was to write a simple account of a simple dog, conveying what she has meant to the small family she joined as a somewhat abused refugee of three years old from the city dog pound, right through to her final weeks and months as a respectably ancient matron of fifteen and a half. In fact, something quite different has emerged. As I have scrutinised Muffin's life in all its apparently ordinary detail – she is, after all, no trick-performing circus dog; she has not rescued people from snowdrifts or leapt nobly into the path of armed robbers and brought them crashing to the ground – I am struck by the depth of its significance. Considering her contribution has taken me to a much broader terrain than I ever anticipated. Yes, this is a journey through 'a dog's life', to use that disparaging phrase, but it has also turned out to be somewhat more than that.

Muffin, it seems, is bigger than the sum of her parts. She came into a household where one member was seriously ill and would die on her watch five years later. She proved to be a great help, if only as a background support, a kind of canine litmus paper, onto which difficult emotions could be safely poured, and spirits miraculously lifted. In short, she always made us feel better. She also helped us to *understand*. So this book is not just about a dog: it is, on another level, a gentle meditation on the quality of life itself. I never intended that – it was all Muffin's work.

One of my favourite drinks is a West Yorkshire tipple called Fentiman's Ginger Beer. This fiery and powerful brew was first developed by a Yorkshire ironworker called Thomas Fentiman in 1905. When approached for a loan by a fellow tradesman, he asked for security on his money, and was given a recipe for botanically brewed ginger beer. The loan was never repaid, so Fentiman kept the recipe as collateral – and built up a lucrative business from door-to-door sales of brewed ginger roots and fragrant herbs. The drink is now a great success, both in the UK and in America. On the label's logo, in pride of place at the top, is Fentiman's prize Alsatian, Fearless, a double winner of Crufts' Obedience Test, and an obvious iconic presence in the life of his owner – so much so that he is now immortalised on every brown beer bottle produced for these shores and well beyond.

Dogs, it seems, are not just individuals; they are also symbols of great devotion, as potent now as they were in the ancient world, when man first tamed them to act as hunters, servants and good companions. The richness of our relationship with dogs – whether ancient or modern – lies in the way that they reflect us back to ourselves. In some strange way, when we look at a dog, we are looking in a mirror. If we are sad, then sadness comes back through the dog's eyes; if we are joyful, then, again, the dog shares our mood. Not all dogs do this to the same degree. There are as many different temperaments in the canine world as there are in the human. The crazy look in the eye of a mistreated fight dog is every bit as alarming as, say, the psychopath recently on the loose in North Leeds, who had a propensity for smashing single women's heads in with a hammer. It does not do to romanticise the animal kingdom. An abused dog, like an abused human, is a creature to be treated with extreme caution and, in the worst cases, simply avoided. That is just common sense. At the more ordinary end of the scale, I believe this to be true: if you treat a dog right, it will repay you with an unbounded flow of loyalty, trust and truthfulness.

Duty is only a part of the story. There is something much more intoxicating wrapped up in the package of the average dog. Dogs give so freely; they cannot help themselves. Indeed, a boundless, profligate enthusiasm is one of the loveliest qualities a dog can offer its owner: the eternal puppy inside the grown-up dog; the traveller's friend, ready for a journey, a game, some aimless recreation, a bit of a lark. A good dog is like that exuberant pal you have – and most of us are blessed with at least one – who manages to radiate all the energy and love for life that spills so easily from happy babies and children but is too often knocked out of us by the gloomier rigours of adulthood.

I know someone, now in his sixties, who has just such an irrepressible spirit. He is a fine musician, a craftsman, a morris dancer, a cheerful wearer of wildly coloured shirts and torn-off jeans and baggy shorts. He is simply the life and soul of every party. The first time I met him, I stared, mesmerised, at his face – not just because of his extraordinary animation, but because he had shaved his moustache and goatee beard in half, north to south, and dyed it bright pink.

In the same way, though switching species, if you choose your dog well, you get this kind of joyfulness every single day. I have been lucky to find this pleasure in the shape of my mongrel, Muffin. She never once, in her heyday, turned down the opportunity to set off with me into the wild blue yonder to see what gentle mischief could be made. She has been a risk-taker in her time and has encouraged me to be one too. Most of all, the motto of her life has been this: 'Wherever you go, I'll go. If things turn out badly, I don't mind. I'm on board, a friend for life. Let's give it a go. Let's have some fun.'

I have never claimed to be a perfect dog owner, any more than I have much clue about relationships or motherhood. Like most of us, I bumble my way through life and simply hope for the best. The best is what I got in Muffin. Only once did I betray her badly. When she was still quite young, she was barking and fussing at my feet to an intolerable degree, over an incident I no longer remember. Something snapped in my mind – no excuses – and I extended my leg and pushed her aggressively across the room. I was only wearing socks, and she was not hurt in any way, but the look in her eyes, of profound shock and disappointment, was almost worse than if I had injured her physically. 'You've let me down,' her expression told me, and I had. The mute dignity in her demeanour, even after being pushed around by someone old enough, and big enough, to know better, was a lesson sharper than a thousand words. I never forgot it. No hand has ever been raised to her in anger, before or since, though a sharp tone of voice is still sometimes necessary, I have to admit.

My dog, in return for very little, has been a source of comfort and consolation in circumstances neither she nor I could ever have foreseen or wanted. An acquaintance of mine, when talking about her own rescue dog, refers to her simply as 'my best friend'. This particular dog has done her own share of therapeutic intervention, when her family have been through horrible disputes and calamities of health and financial hardship. Friendship, in the form of reliable, non-judgemental, warm and humorous companionship, is the most precious of resources in anyone's life. Muffin has been my friend too, in animal incarnation – one of the best I have had, and one whose unswerving devotion I will find it hard to replicate ever again.

Telling the story of Muffin's life – beginning towards the end, but encapsulating everything special along the way, in what has been a truly remarkable canine journey – is both a privilege and a pleasure. If I have put words in her mouth and thoughts in her head that she might not recognise, then I apologise to the dog – I am only human, after all.

The story starts in autumn 2011. Muffin has already been seriously and repeatedly ill in the months leading up to this. But, as the following weeks unfold, I find out – to my delight and constant astonishment – that there is much more life in the old dog yet.

Chapter One

Somewhere Towards the End

When my daughter was a baby, I would creep into her bedroom at night while she slept and hover by her cot, just to listen to her breathing. There was something consoling in that gentle sound – and reassuring for an anxious first-time mother. Those little snores and snuffles were proof of her vitality and health. She was still alive, still safe. I had managed, somehow, to steer the little creature through another twenty-four hours.

These days I find myself on a similar mission with my dog. Although only a modest-sized mutt, Muffin has been a prodigious snorer in her time, her rib-heaving groans reverberating through doors and walls. These days, her breath is like a whisper, a faint echo of its former self. Unlike my then baby daughter, Muffin is not at the beginning but right at the end of her life. Each time she breathes these days, the movements ripple awkwardly along her body in punctuated waves of effort. Each inhalation is a victory; every exhalation a welcome release. Watching her is like witnessing the beautiful bare mechanics of life itself, stretched out before me on the carpet, covered in fur.

I am reminded of a television news interview from a couple of years back, recorded on Midsummer's Day at Stonehenge, down among the Druids.

Interviewer: 'Why do you come here and celebrate like this? What's it all about?'

Young female interviewee (gazing in wonder at a cloudy dawn sky): 'One breath in, one breath out. It's all we've got.'

At the time I laughed at her pretension. Now I understand.

It is 2011. In a couple of weeks' time, my daughter Molly leaves for university. The ordinary world that I inhabit, in a tiny household of three – dog, daughter and me – is all undone. Molly, of course, will return from time to time: her flight from the nest is a joyful expansion, a creative leap. Muffin, sick and slowly fading, will be gone for good. Despite all the losses I have sustained over the years, the deaths and long illnesses of people close to me, the end is always a shock, an assault to the senses – one I am never prepared for, and one I will do almost anything to put off until tomorrow, for tomorrow, as we know, never comes.

Writer Mary Oliver, in a tribute to her lost, beloved, dark-haired dog, in the poem 'Her Grave', says how fortunate you are if your dog makes it to fifteen. Muffin is three months short of that mark. It is twelve years since we scooped her up from the RSPCA dog pound in Leeds and brought her home, a mangy little rescue mongrel, then three years old and woefully mis-treated – just a pair of big eyes with a skeleton attached. She has lived on borrowed time ever since.

When the vet first checked her over, he signalled an early warning. 'The heartbeat is fast and irregular. She's fine now, but it could be a problem later on.'

In fact, Muffin tore her reckless way through the next decade without cardiac arrest or heart-related incident of any kind. This was all the more remarkable given the speed she ran, the heights she scaled – and depths she unwittingly plumbed, from sea walls to small reservoirs, hurtling into the water below – as she pointed her snout defiantly towards the distant horizon. For the first three years of her life, before she was rescued, she had apparently been confined to a high-rise flat, and was never let out for exercise or play. So, at the first hint of fresh air and the sight of open spaces, she was off, and nothing was going to stop her.

Ultimately, however, the vet's prophecy did come true. By the summer of 2009, she had developed an intermittent but trou-blesome cough. In 2010, when the cough had developed into bouts of wheezing and choking – even fainting fits, which left her gasping for breath and stretched out on the floor, semi-conscious – heart disease was confirmed. Since then, the words 'VET'S APPOINTMENT' appear with alarming regularity in my diary. She is on so many different potions and pills, she practically rattles every time she stands up. This year so far she has survived a near drowning, partially dislocated her hip – now mended – and suffered a minor stroke and its aftermath. In addition, she has an enlarged heart, congested capillaries, cataracts on both eyes, increasing deafness and a large dose of daftness, memory loss and pronounced geriatric eccentricity. But she is still here.

Summer is over and September has arrived. The days are growing shorter; the light is softer and more elusive. There is a nip in the air, a sense of something inexorable on the horizon, a closing-in. Ironically, this cool tang, the first flag of defeat from the passing year, seems to suit the dog. After a long and groggy August, when it could be an effort just to get her on her feet and outside the door, she has developed almost a spring in her step, at least for a few precious moments every day. After a long break, we are back into a familiar routine of two short walks a day in the little wood at the end of our road.

Just when I think the game is up, Muffin gives herself a reprieve. Is it for her or for me? 'I think she'll stick around until Molly has gone to university, don't you?' said a friend. She'll stay to keep me company, or maybe she is just not ready to go yet. Despite the cataracts, those eyes are still a bit shiny and bright, and the greed for her supper remains. All the same, it feels as if we have come a full and complete circle in the story of Muffin's life.

First, we – her adopted family – were the rescuers, starting her off on a happy new adventure after a nasty start of near star-vation and neglect. It did not take her long to recover. Soon she thrived and then *she* became the nurse, helping my husband through a long illness with her constant, kind companionship.

After his death, she turned her stewardship to my daughter and me, steering us through a minefield of grief, into the tunnel of bereavement and out the other side, back into the light. She was a playmate for my daughter and a cheerful chore to me. The long walks kept me healthy; the dog's sense of humour made me smile. Now, once again, it is our turn to hold her up – sometimes literally – when she loses her balance and falls. This at least she is owed: a graceful and dignified finish.

Anyone who has ever had dealings with dogs will know no two canines are in any way alike. As with humans, they come in a bewildering array of shapes, sizes, colours and temperaments. And, like our human offspring, they do not always turn out the way we might expect.

Back in 1999, sitting in the waiting room of the RSPCA rescue centre, leafing through the information on the dogs available, I didn't have much of an idea what I was looking for. The job description was simple enough: a happy, furry companion for my seven-year-old daughter; a chance for my husband, already terminally ill with cancer, to have a dog of his own, something he had always wanted but thus far never achieved; and an opportunity for me to relive some funny and sweet childhood memories of the crazy little mongrel that I grew up alongside. Beyond that, ideas of breed, appearance and character were immaterial (which is just as well, given the shocking state Muffin arrived in – a neurotic, shivering little shipwreck of a dog; not promising). But we were lucky and we chose well.

After a hair-raising couple of weeks – barging into furniture, scratching at doors and pooing on the carpet indiscriminately – Muffin soon lived up to her brief for all three of us. In her company, Molly overcame childhood nerves around animals to become her greatest friend and ally. Tim simply fell in love with her, and now I am falling further. But there was more. The dog, it seems, had a deeper agenda than any of us had bargained for: just as surely as we selected her, she selected us.

The first time she clapped eyes on the three of us, she headed straight for Tim. This was odd, because she was a mere scrap of a thing at the time – the slightest hint of a breeze would have blown her away – and Tim was a strapping man of six foot five, with a deep voice and an imposing manner. Nonetheless, she shot directly at him, jumping at his legs over and over, as if to say, 'I've got him! This one's mine!'

Their connection was not without its problems: he was house-proud and unused to the chaos of a new dog, and she was wary of men. If she misbehaved in the early days, Tim would bellow and Muffin would run for cover, but the bond between them quickly grew strong. She walked with him in the good times; she lay by his bed in the bad. She was always at his side. Even when he was admitted to the local hospice, Muffin was a frequent visitor. She stayed overnight when the end was close. She was protective, steadfast, unflinching. She remains that way today, with her two remaining family members, a duty of care hardwired into her little frame, belying her unpromising, wasted beginnings.

The loyalty of dogs towards their human masters is undisputed and legendary. They became domesticated millennia ago, before any other animal – horse, cow or pig. Dog was top. Nor was it just about the work that they did, as guard dogs, farm hands, sheep herders or load bearers. The bond was always stronger, somehow more enmeshed – even spiritual – than that.

I grew up on the story of Greyfriars Bobby, the little Skye terrier from the Victorian era who for years walked out on the Edinburgh beat with his policeman master, John Gray, come rain or shine. When Gray died of tuberculosis, Bobby attended his funeral. That night he returned to the burial plot, lying on top of the freshly dug earth to keep vigil. He was shooed away but returned to the grave the following day – and the day after that – for the next fourteen years, until his own death in 1872. With his master gone, he refused ever to leave the churchyard again.

A year or so after my husband Tim had died, I travelled to Ireland to visit some mutual friends and – according to his wishes – scattered some of his ashes in their garden. He had a detailed list of where his remains were to be sprinkled, leaving the spirit of himself, like largesse, in many of his best-loved places. Such meticulous forward planning was true to his nature as a supremely organised and yet rather romantic man.

Our friends had a rescue dog too. Pickles was well known for her humour and kindness – and her uncanny ability to pick up on moods and atmospheres, to 'be alongside' the humans she knew. So she recognised immediately the importance of the occasion, even though it was low key and relatively light-hearted. After the

ashes had been scattered – behind a bush in the long border – and
the toast given, Pickles lay down on a stretch of grass nearby and
refused to move. 'That's odd, she never lies there,' said her
owners. But there she stayed. I left the next day. Apparently
Pickles went back to the same spot in the evening and lay down.
She repeated the ritual every day for a week, honouring an
absence without even knowing who had left.

Muffin, I know, is by no means unique amongst dogs for her
empathy, her courtesy and care, but the subtlety and power of
her response to the people around her can still astonish me.
When she was young, she started to cough and sneeze during the
summer months, when the grass was high and the pollen count
bothersome.

'Does anyone in the family have hay fever?' the vet asked,
casually enough.

'Yes, my daughter does. Why?' I replied.

He shrugged. 'It's not uncommon for dogs to mimic their
owners' symptoms.'

As Molly has got older, her hay fever has diminished. Now
Muffin doesn't sneeze in the summer any more.

Still, she can detect sadness through the thickest of doors and
walls and she will lie in wait to offer the sufferer consolation.
Once, when we had to stop the car, so that Tim – stuffed full of
his cancer drugs – could get to the side of the road to vomit, the
dog, sitting on a friend's lap, began to retch violently at exactly
the same moment that Tim was sick. I have no explanation for
these responses.

I have little experience of such a sensitive dog. The mongrel I grew up with was a wild, untutored terrier-crossbreed. She was fast, she was zany and she was noisy. There was always someone shouting in our large and bolshie family, and Tess shouted the loudest. When we travelled by car, she would whine and pace and pant and slaver from the minute she got in to the minute she leapt out at the other end. She jumped into deep water at the drop of a hat, could swim like a fish and showed off like a crazy clown. I talked to her all the time – but never once imagined that she was listening. In truth, I don't think she really was. Tess was a joyful bundle of energy and she followed her own star. She liked us all well enough, but that was as far as it went. Her selfishness was supreme, her prime concern her own satisfaction. And why not? Still, the difference between Tess and Muffin in this regard is as great as it could possibly be.

Just a short walk through the local wood confirms that the idiosyncrasies of the humans are perfectly matched by the quirks of their pets. There is kind and friendly Sam, the Border collie, who calls out a voluble greeting as soon as he sees anyone he knows, whether they have two legs or four, and invariably comes stepping up to meet me, tall tail waving, like a gracious host at a country house. Then there's cheerful Chester, head of a gang of three and the oldest in his tribe, who runs ahead to check out the territory and wears his badge of responsibility like a well-scrubbed head boy. Sometimes we see nervous little Maggie, the small, silky-eared King Charles spaniel, or old fella Bounce, stiff-legged and all of eighteen years old, but still on for a bit of a wander with his best friend and companion, the shy blonde Puppy Dog. Then there are various rescued greyhounds, thin as rakes, and wrapped up warm against the weather, shepherded carefully along the way by their ever-solicitous owners. Rottweilers, Dobermanns, Tibetan terriers, pitbulls – it's a very small wood, but it's teeming with life.

Some of the dogs shy away instinctively; others are confident and extrovert. The good-looking males hold their heads and tails up high for display. The pretty females, as Muffin once was, skitter around them in circles and show off outrageously. The flirting and the fighting, the friendships and the fallings-out – everything is on open display, whilst the humans look on in bemusement, like indulgent and anxious parents at the nursery door. What will their offspring get up to next? Twelve years we have been walking here, my dog and I, and we have seen several generations of canines come and go. All, at one time, have been running and sparring, firm – or fleeting – companions for Muffin.

Death, when it happens to these dogs, is not always kind or gentle. One spaniel was poisoned by contaminated food thrown down under the trees to kill the rats. A large and lovely lurcher-type (one of Muffin's favourites) was given too much anaesthetic by the vet for a minor operation and simply never woke up. Several have been run over; others attacked. One pitbull was even abducted – possibly for illegal dogfights, a vicious and lucrative underground activity. (Since he was ill and on medication, he may have died before he made his kidnappers any money at all. He has certainly never been found.) The thing I dread most is seeing a regular dog walker on his or her own in the wood, because always they come as a unit – walker and dog. If there is a solitary human, walking head down through the trees, it can mean only one thing: the dog is sick, or the dog has died. I am aware that, sooner or later, one of those sad, lonely walkers will be me.

Muffin regards Gipton Wood as entirely her own. It is a place she loves and has known all her (rescued) life, where she feels completely comfortable, at home. Whenever we have travelled and have finally landed back, the wood is the first place she returns to, in an ecstasy of relief and satisfaction. The relish of the familiar smells, the tread of the stick-strewn, winding paths, the tangle of brambles in the middle dip, and the fallen dead tree trunks at the far quiet corner, the bracken, the bluebells, holly-bush and rowan, old oaks and beech, the masses of grey squirrels to chase and the nesting birds to dislodge and disturb: this is pure heaven for a little dog, and delightful for the owners besides.

Some of Tim's ashes are here too, under an old tree, dis-creetly strewn, for when he was well the wood was his proud dominion and the woodland flowers his abiding pleasure. We pass by the spot each morning and I usually have a quiet word. (That's what a dog does for you – it gives you permission to be a little weird. Talking out loud alone would be taboo; with a dog at your feet, it's fine.)

Muffin has mislaid herself in these surroundings many a time before and found her way home happily. She even set off from the house on her own on a couple of occasions, exasperated by my unreasonable delays and desperate for a morning pee. I saw her once, from the bedroom window, trotting back up the road, sticking obediently to the path like a human pedestrian – mission accomplished. She is so familiar with this wood, treating it like her back garden through the years, that I knew something was seriously wrong in March this year when she got lost one morning and didn't make it back.

Old dogs walk slowly. They dawdle; they ponder. They sniff, sniff, sniff. When Muffin was younger, we would fly around the paths together, passing on our way several owners, who were invariably standing and waiting, while their aged pets did their interminable, stationary business. Used to being permanently on the move, pressing forward in a rush, with Muffin bounding through the trees in front of me, this form of static exercise seemed incomprehensible.

How patient these people were, but how could they stand the boredom? One man explained, watching indulgently as his dog buried her nose endlessly in the same thicket of old grass, 'I don't mind really. This is her time in here. I'm happy to let her be.' But I was sure that, when the time came, I would not be so measured and forgiving. I was also arrogant and naive enough to think that it never *would* come. Now here we are and I was right: since Muffin has joined the ranks of the ones who linger rather than run, the whole thing drives me wild with frustration.

On this particular afternoon in March, I was striding ahead

in my customary fashion, confident that Muffin would catch me up in the end, as she always did. In fact, I had glanced back only minutes before and had seen her ambling close behind me. Then, suddenly, she was gone. I turned on the path towards home, calling her name. Nothing. This is the day I learned two things: how deaf she had become and how easily disorientated. It did not take long for panic to set in. Like letting go of a child's hand in a large supermarket and then seeing a blank space where the child once was, the world just fell away. I ran through the entire wood, screaming like a banshee. Had anyone seen her? They hadn't. It occurred to me, in my confusion, that she might have made it back home, so I laboured up the road and checked there. Nothing. If she went out onto the main Roundhay Road – an endless flow of fast-moving traffic at the bottom end of the wood – I knew she would be finished. Back into the trees I charged, and bumped into a man with a large dog on a lead.

'I've seen her,' he said. 'I think my dog frightened her. She ran back that way.'

He pointed to the most remote corner of the wood and I pounded up the path, not thinking for a moment she would still be there, as it was a full fifteen minutes after her encounter with him, but she was. Standing on the path, stock still, she looked utterly confused – quite unable to go forward or back – and surrounded by an invisible bubble of isolation. It was the loneliest thing I have ever seen.

Since that day, I keep her always on an extendable lead, and do my best to tolerate the long pauses between movement and the constant rewinding and untangling process, as she wraps the long wire round yet another bush. The curtailment of her freedom, in favour of her safety, was a hard decision to make and a confirmation of a new chapter in her life. She was officially an old dog now.

Some dogs love water and others hate it. Muffin is in another category altogether: she despises the wet. If it rains, she would rather not go outside at all. She hates getting her face wet and would rather have all her fur shaved off than go for a bath. Despite this, she has an unerring instinct (or death wish), which has drawn her, over and over through the years, towards deep water. Unfortunately for me – since it is usually me who has had to rescue her, by jumping in or dragging her to safety, getting covered in slime or sea water in the process – Muffin often chooses nearly to drown herself in the middle of winter.

If March's incident in the wood was confirmation of her encroaching senility, then the month before provided an early warning signal almost fatal in its consequences. The winter had been bitter and long. Temperatures dropped so consistently low that an inch of sheet ice lay over our road for weeks, making walking both perilous and foolhardy. We live on a hill, and cannot find a flat surface anywhere. In the past, I relied on Muffin to pull me up a slope when the going got tough. She is a small enough dog, but was always sturdy, her four short legs a distinct advantage in slippery terrain over my two long spindly ones. Last winter, the tables were turned. The dog's hind legs are withered now with age and arthritis, so much so that her back end hardly seems to belong to the front, and the propulsion and balance in her hips is seriously compromised.

The frozen surfaces of February were a nightmare for her. She slid around like a drunk in an ice rink – and I wasn't a great deal better. Several times, on our abbreviated walks, I was reduced to dropping on all fours and crawling along, stopping from time to time to hoick the dog beside me. So it was a relief – and a welcome return to some dignity for both of us – when the thaw came. With it came high winds and storms, but we were desperate to get out and go further than the end of our road, so we took a chance on the blustery weather and drove up to the local park.

Roundhay Park in Leeds is a justifiable source of civic pride and joy. A rich man's plaything in the nineteenth century, it was turned over to the city by Thomas Nicholson in 1871. There were spectacular events throughout the Victorian era – pageants on the water and tightrope walking over the ravine – whilst in modern times, the great grass amphitheatre that lies at the park's centre has been host to some legendary rock events: the Rolling Stones, Bruce Springsteen, Michael Jackson, Madonna, Robbie Williams . . . And every year people flock from miles around to see the massive bonfire and firework display on the high expanse of Soldiers' Fields and Hill 60. Muffin, however, prefers quieter pleasures. There are three stretches of water in the park. Given her track record, it is remarkable that she has never fallen in any of them – until now.

Waterloo Lake is Roundhay's glittering set piece. Named in honour of the soldiers newly returned from the Napoleonic Wars, who were given the work of constructing the foundations of the lake, it measures 18 metres deep and 33 metres across. It is a serene, light-filled expanse of water, with reflections of tree, sun and sky on a clear day. In her prime, Muffin would race tirelessly up the woodland slopes surrounding the water, and track the progress of whoever was walking with her by running down from time to time, and darting backwards and forwards along the narrow lakeside pathway to round up her people. She always veered dangerously close to the water's edge on her countless descents from the high line of trees – only my loud cries of alarm making her brake in the nick of time. Spatial awareness, apparently, is not a spaniel's strong point. It is the spaniel in Muffin that makes her weave around people's ankles, tripping them up, making them curse. The collie in her makes her roam and run in ever-increasing circles. Neither breed seems to know quite when to STOP and CONSIDER, so a combination of both is lethal.

As the dog has grown older, two shorter alternative routes through the park have had to be found. One is along the gorge and ravine, on a high bank that follows a flow of water crossing boulders and gullies deep below. Muffin used to love to run along this dirt bank at full pelt. She never chose the centre of the path but always its vertiginous edge, where the earth drops away in a steep descent to the stream. I wonder if she ever sensed and relished the danger? Was she playing with gravity, responding to some deep-felt desire to leave the ground entirely, to fly? Or was she just blissfully unaware? She never actually fell into the ravine, but there was many a scramble to stop a painful tumble and avert disaster. Now Muffin is officially elderly, we take the shortest and most sedate route of all: around the small and quiet Upper Lake. The ground is flat and the path, for the most part, is a discreet distance away from the water's edge.

This is the path we took in February, in the wake of the winter storms. Muffin was already becoming a little erratic. On our walks, she was taking longer to respond to my calls, which were, in turn, becoming much more shrill and emphatic, but nothing was amiss this particular morning. As usual, I was walking a few paces ahead. Muffin had found some devastatingly interesting scent in a copse of trees to our left. One of these trees, prey to the recent wild weather, had fallen smack across the main path. I stepped over it and carried on, calling for the dog to catch me up. I assumed she would run around the tree at the point where its roots had been ripped from the ground – the point furthest from the water, and nearest to where she was standing and sniffing. Instead, she suddenly ran the entire length of the tree trunk, expecting to find land at the end of it and a place to cut round and join me on the other side, but what she found was a sheer drop into the lake more than 2 metres below her. She plummeted. One second I saw her running; the next, she had vanished into thin air.

I ran to the edge of the water and peered below. I saw a tiny grass ledge – the only dry patch anywhere on the lake's lower perimeter – and Muffin had landed, with her arthritic legs somehow intact, on that. She hates water, but she can swim. She was pacing back and forth on the outcrop, and then plunging into the water on either side, doggy-paddling with panic. If she started to swim further out, in her bid to escape, she would soon exhaust herself and drown. I kept calling her back to the dry, but she was becoming more and more confused. She couldn't see me from below, and her hearing was impaired and non-directional. The drop was too sheer for me to manage on my own. If I got down, I would never get out. So I did what I always do when the dog is in an emergency: I shouted, 'Help!' with rising hysteria. In most situations, I remain calm, at least to the world outside, but when it comes to the dog, I am immediately undone.

A young woman ran to me. We both peered down. The dog was still churning around in ever-decreasing circles. A second person bounded up, two dogs running at his sides. The man was huge, his accent East European. I asked if he would help me down.

'No!' he boomed, his hand firmly gesturing me to stop. 'I'll go!'

With reckless disregard for his own safety, he jumped down to the water in a single beat, scooped the soaking Muffin up in his arms and deposited her, shivering and gasping, onto the grass above. Then he bounced up and down on his feet, hooked his elbows over the high bank and scrambled back to terra firma himself. I was struck with awe at his spontaneous kindness, his strong and swift action.

'Thank you so much,' I stammered. 'My dog would have died if you hadn't come along.'

He rubbed his wet, mucky arms down his jeans and shrugged. 'We love our dogs,' he said, and was gone.

The way that people talk about their dogs is simple and direct, straight to the heart. Often I know the names of the animals I see on my regular walks, but not their owners'. It doesn't matter. Human ego – briefly, mercifully – is put to one side, as we share profoundly unimportant details about our dogs' food – 'Have you tried raw carrot? It's very good for their teeth', 'My dog loves peas . . . She eats them like sweeties' – or exercise routines, beds and baths, whilst actually confessing to something much deeper and elemental. We are talking about love. The connection to these companion dogs is a profoundly nourishing one, full of pleasure and vitality. They are, in a sense, the baby offspring who never grow up and leave home. As Muffin's heroic Slavonic rescuer put it so succinctly, we love our dogs – and not in the complicated, tortuous, self-doubting way that we love our fellow humans. The love of a dog is more primitive, somehow purer, certainly simpler, and their attachment to *us* is even more so.

In his book *In Defence of Dogs*, biologist John Bradshaw has a chapter entitled 'Does Your Dog Love You?' Through the centuries, dogs' domestication has taught them to have intense emotional attachments to their owners. A study carried out in South Africa, reports Bradshaw, documented a series of friendly interactions carried out human to dog. During these episodes, when the dogs were stroked, patted and played with one to one, the dogs' levels of oxytocin (a hormone released in women before birth – the nurturing hormone) rose fivefold. Endorphin and dopamine levels – the feel-good factors – doubled, and the dogs' blood pressure dropped significantly. In other words, when we are kind to dogs, we do them a great deal of good; they thrive. Writes Bradshaw, 'Happiness – joy – seems to radiate from the majority of dogs, much of the time. Happy dogs have relaxed, open faces, and bodies that wiggle from the shoulders backwards, including the tail . . .' They have a natural optimism and zest. Do dogs love us? Of course they do.

Where love is concerned, there can be treachery too – at least on the human side of the equation. Now that my daughter is flying the nest and I am often left alone with my ancient mongrel, curled up in her basket and fixing me with her baleful eye, I can't help but think how much freer I will be when she is gone. It is ironic. Just as I am released from the fourteen-year tyranny of the school day, the pleading entreaties to 'Get your homework done!', the packing of lunches at seven in the morning and the mercy trips in the car to pick up my child at the school gate in the pouring rain – just as all that goes, another kind of servitude arises. Muffin is too old to walk far, does not really like to travel these days and is increasingly hard to leave with other people. (Who knows when she might pee – or worse – on the carpet, have a coughing fit and faint, fall over and not be able to get up again?)

The young adult daughter has gone and the elderly dog is more dependent than ever. Delicious Empty Nester thoughts of taking a road trip, or a quick four days abroad, during term time and on my own, are banished. Duty still calls. Life these days is a complicated mixture of pain and regret that the dog is so manifestly failing – albeit with periods of sweet remission – added to a sense of what lies beyond, the wide-open spaces of dog-free possibilities.

'But you'll have another one, surely?' My dog-lover friends are convinced. 'You'll miss her so much, especially now that Molly is going away.'

Despite what other people may think, I know in my heart I'll have one dog and one dog only. Muffin is the one. In the same way, Tess was the dog of my childhood. When I left home for university, the last of three children to fly the coop, my parents were left with each other and an aged dog. Tess staggered on for another four years. I remember the phone call from my mother when I was taking my finals. 'Don't cry,' she said, ineffectually, as she gave me the news that Tess was dead. They never had another dog after that. Tess entered the realm of reminiscence and fond family legend: the naughty dog who got away with everything, all the time.

Life comes full circle, and unconscious parallels are at work. Molly was the same age when Muffin arrived in our family as I was when we got Tess: seven years old. Now university and the big wide world beckon her. Muffin herself is now fifteen years old – the same age Tess was when she died. And, like my mother before me, I have decided after this one, no more. In the end, the bond is too confining, and the prospect of it ending too painful.

Nearly drowned and almost lost – Muffin's start to this, her fifteenth year, was certainly a chaotic and debilitated one. The contrast she made to the newer, younger dogs on the block was becoming more and more marked. Friends of ours had acquired a Tibetan terrier. We tried, in the early days after his arrival, to use Muffin as a calm and socialising influence, but the puppy was just too Tigger-like. Muffin felt cornered and intimidated. On shared walks in the wood, he wanted to play, to bounce, to run; Muffin just wanted to hide.

In April, there was a trip north to a family wedding. During a big celebration dinner beforehand, Muffin started to choke and fit. She went into spasm and then she fainted. By then, I was used to these occasional dramatic bouts – a nasty side-effect of the problems with her heart – but the alarm it caused to everyone else was palpable. They were used to a very different animal – as fit as a flea, and twice as lively. Tom, the paramedic-in-waiting amongst us, jumped to red alert, but mouth-to-mouth resuscitation, with Muffin's disgusting, old-dog breath, would have been an ordeal, to say the least. Luckily she revived before it came to that.

Tom himself has a young rescue dog, called Jools. She is beautiful, lively, full of joy. The following day we went for a walk on a wide Northumbrian beach. Jools pounded the surf and sailed after her ball tirelessly; she danced, she dived, she span round and round in circles of delight. Muffin, on the other hand, plodded slowly at my side, safe at the end of her extendable lead, one paw ponderously placed in front of the other, showing not the slightest air of interest in Jools's extended acrobatics.

Despite the difference in their looks – one dog black and shaggy, the other short-haired and white, with honey-coloured patches – the behaviour of both seemed poignantly connected, like before and after photographs come to life. In Jools I saw the young dog Muffin, running wild as a whippet on beach holidays the length and breadth of the country, when my daughter was young and Tim was still with us. In Muffin I saw just herself, right now, grown old and slow and increasingly indifferent, worn out.

Spring turned to summer, slowly, wistfully, in what was a strange and defining year for our small family. A-level exam season descended on my daughter. School timetables were suspended. Endless revision loomed. A gloomy, bookish pall settled over the whole house. The date of her last exam was Tuesday, 21 June: the summer solstice, maximum light. I decided to have a celebration for the return of the brightest, longest day.

On the Sunday before, I went downstairs early, as usual, to take the dog for her walk. Something about her seemed strange and unsteady. She looked at me from her basket, all out of focus, pitching her milky gaze somewhere to the right of where I was standing. When she tried to get up, she fell over. Her back legs kept collapsing. When I got closer, I noticed that her eyes were flicking rapidly from side to side. She was not herself: this was a contorted shell of the dog I had said goodnight to the previous day. Somehow, we made it to the woods. I thought her hips were displaced and was testing whether she could walk at all. Soon I was holding her up, supporting her between my legs when hers refused to work. I got her home, convinced the game was up.

I knew this for a fact: if the back end of a dog goes, and it cannot stand or walk, then there is nothing that can be done. Already I was rehearsing the end in my head, whilst carefully shielding my daughter from the news, exam-exhausted as she was and up to her eyes in last-minute revision notes. I did not want the dog to see an emergency Sunday vet, so I kept her quiet that day, carried her in her basket up to my bedroom overnight, and woke every hour or so through the night, to watch her lying in a semi-collapsed state, eyes open and flicking madly.

'Just make it till morning,' I thought. 'Keep going till then.'

The next morning, I booked her in to the usual vet, and rang for extra homeopathic advice, as this system of complementary care had worked well in crises with the dog before. The homeopath was precise and accurate, even over the phone. I explained what was happening with her eyes. 'I don't think it is her legs,' he said firmly. 'I think she has had a stroke. She is falling over because her sense of balance has gone.' He prescribed some homeopathic remedies to help the dizziness settle.

In the late afternoon, I took her to her vet, the friendly and sympathetic Neil. He confirmed, 'It's a stroke.' The little dog stood in the middle of the consulting room, back legs sliding away from her, head listing to the right, body twisted every which way, trying to hold herself together, and looking like a lost cause if ever I saw one. But I had seen that look before, way back when we first rescued her, and I was determined to try and rescue her again.

The vet injected her with steroids and sounded a note of mixed hope and caution. 'Keep her quiet, keep her cool. She mustn't walk, except supported, into the garden, to do her business. She may recover completely; she may have another stroke. There's no way of knowing which way it will go. Just take her home and look after her.' So I did.

I cancelled the upcoming party. I turned the hall into a kind of dog nursery, with sheets and screens to keep out the sun and soft cushions to stop her bumping into sharp edges. I half-carried, half-led her outside for the occasional pee. She neither slept nor moved much; she simply endured. For hours on end, she hung off the edge of her basket, her head dropping awkwardly to one side. My respect for her suffering, and the capacity to tolerate her own discomfort and distress, shot through the ceiling. She was a fighter – that was certain. Still, I was convinced, in my heart, that she wouldn't make it. The weight of that knowledge felt suffocating.

For years I have resented the daily walks, cursing the need to go out in the dark, in the rain, early in the morning, late at night, to give the dog her necessary exercise. It is lovely to be outside, and we are fortunate to have a wood on our doorstep, but I have been unnecessarily grumpy about the whole process, the tyranny of the routine. Suddenly, released from that chore, and told firmly NOT to walk the dog under any circumstances, I felt irresistibly compelled to go walking on my own.

I left the dog with my daughter and slipped out to the woods, half-walking, half-running, not knowing where I was going or why. I ended up at the holly tree where I always talked to Tim. Only this time I said nothing at all and, for the first time, he 'talked' back. I stood with my back to the tree and felt his hands on my shoulders – a palpable presence – swaying me softly from side to side. 'Bring her to me,' said a voice in my head. I knew what it meant: bring her ashes to the tree should Muffin not survive her stroke, so that the connection between the man and the dog could be honoured and concluded. There was no comfort in this encounter, pulled up, as it must have been, deep from my own subconscious. I do not believe in ghosts, in the afterlife, in 'voices' and omens. But something happened in that moment. Crisis creates an otherworldly strangeness – and I have never had a stranger experience than this one.

They say that every death, every significant loss, contains within it the sum of all other losses in your life. And that the relationship you have with the lost person – or animal, indeed – does not necessarily correspond to the depth of your emotion. Somehow, each bereavement, or even the threat of one, becomes more and more profound: the elastic keeps getting a little thinner. Whilst it would be absurd to say that the feeling engendered by Muffin's stroke was in any way equivalent to the grief at losing my husband, my mother or my father (who himself died of a catastrophic stroke just over a year ago), there *was* a sense in which everyone who had been taken from me in recent years became suddenly illuminated through the dog's sudden suffering, and wrapped in a fresh and heavy sadness. I really was not ready for this little dog to die. And thankfully she didn't.

Slowly, as the hours went by, on the day following her attack, it became clear that the medication was beginning to work. Something started to settle behind the dog's eyes. The storm in her brain quietened down. She still staggered when she walked, her head still tilted and dropped to the right, but she was definitely pulling through.

'I think this dog is on better form than she was before the stroke,' the vet exclaimed, a few days later, with a touching delight. And he was right. There was a clarity in her demeanour, a renewed alacrity in her step. Of course, this could have been helped by me misreading the label on the bottle of pills, and giving her double the amount of steroids that she had been prescribed for the first two weeks. She had a phase of bounding through the woods after that, like an East German shot-putter fresh from behind the Iron Curtain. Let's just call it a medically enhanced high. It didn't last, but it was clear, once again, that Muffin was a formidable survivor. She wasn't through with us yet.

July floated away like a dream. Muffin and I kept our heads

down and stayed quiet. My daughter finished her A levels and
left school. We were all cut loose from our moorings then: three
kites drifting in a wide sky. Molly went away to London for a
holiday. I stayed at home with the dog. I did take Muffin on one
trip south, to family and friends. The old dog sprawled on the
back seat all around the M25 in baking-hot weather – the one
heatwave of the summer, which lasted all of three days. I kept
a beady eye on her through the rear-view mirror, watching for
the telltale rise and fall of her belly, looking for the reassurance
of old lungs still pressed into action. It was a bit of a stretch for
her to do this travelling, and when she got back she had prolonged diarrhoea from the stress – another warning shot across
the bows. Before long, I thought, we would be confined to the
house and the few metres it took to get to the back garden. Our
world was getting alarmingly small.

People who had not seen Muffin in a while were startled by
the change in her over the summer. 'She doesn't even know me,'
cried my cousin, one of Muffin's biggest fans and a faithful
dogsitter down the years. The dog's bewilderment and disorientation had left her numbed, even to people she had felt a
strong attachment to for a long, long time.

'It's nothing personal,' I wanted to say, but that would only
make things worse. Because that very detachment of extreme old
age, when the world is reduced to a solipsistic round of eating
and sleeping, feels like an insult to those who are still engaged,
still connected to the one who is slowly leaving. It is nothing of
the kind, of course.

My dad was a humorous man. As he got older, the humour became ever more mordant and mischievous. He traded on his physical frailty, which concealed a mind as sharp as a razor right up to the moment of his stroke, to mock the robustness and greed of the commercial world around him. 'Times are hard,' he would say, shaking his head sadly, at the cold meats counter, when he came to stay with me in Leeds. 'Do the best that you can.' The poor shop assistant, shocked by his candour, would invariably slip in a few extra slices of ham and hand them over with a sympathetic smile. Dad's eyes would glint in triumph, as he leaned on his stick heavily to walk away. Whilst never a rich man, he was not particularly short of money, he just liked a practical joke. In the end, I banned him from coming shopping with me altogether. Then there was the time he 'forgot' to pay for the desserts, when he took us out for lunch at the local pub, and was chased by a flustered barman all the way to our car. 'So sorry, my mistake,' Dad said, with an insouciant smile, as he graciously agreed to pay up.

Muffin lacks the calculation of my father, but she has always been a comical little dog. In her time, she relished games and funny jokes – dressing up and hide-and-seek, running to chase and jumping to catch, dodging backwards and forwards round tight corners and sharp bends, faster and faster, just for the fun of feeling herself move. As she has got older, the humour is of a less intentional kind. Her spatial awareness is now non-existent. She wanders aimlessly through the house from time to time, squeezing herself into tiny spaces, getting stuck behind tables and chairs and pushing her head into bookcases, knocking over lamps. Unable to employ her former stealth, she invariably gives herself away as the kitchen bin crashes to the floor yet again, during clumsy attempts at thieving the chicken carcass or empty ready-meal cartons. She is a pilferer – always has been. Rescue dogs are hungry dogs, and she is constantly on the lookout for an illicit bite. Random peeing and pooing is also becoming a problem. Muffin has always been a creature of habit – reliable bowels at regular times – but not any more. Most of this I forgive, even if sometimes it feels a little wilful.

In the summer my daughter and I had to be photographed for an article in the newspaper. The photographer left his expensive gear behind him on the grass, as he moved in closer for a portrait shot. Somehow, Muffin managed to escape from the kitchen and could be seen listing slowly into view, making her creaky way over to the pile of equipment. Mid-shot, mid-smile, unable to move, I saw her squat down and deposit a little prize, literally inches away from the cameraman's precious lenses. Having made her point, she simply wandered off again and lay down at the far end of the lawn. Later in the summer, we paid a visit to my nephew's new house. It was pristine inside, with a clean and tidy patio outside. Muffin walked to the middle of the patio, squatted down and peed luxuriantly, never mind that she had been taken for a long walk only an hour before. Old age: a licence to behave badly. My father knew that and it seems that the dog is following happily in his footsteps.

'I dread the day when I have to make that decision,' said the owner of an old dog, who walks in the woods. She was talking about the decision to end a dog's life, the call many of us have to make eventually, in the name of humanity and simple kindness. Muffin is not in pain. She still likes a walk. She still loves her food. She still responds to the world around her in a way that betrays a level of satisfaction and well-being. When that changes substantially, I hope that I will know. I hope, too, that I am brave enough to say 'Enough'. Since the dog cannot speak, however, there will always be a shadow of doubt, which can be haunting.

Author Penny Vincenzi talked about this in a women's magazine, describing her saddest decision as 'asking the vet to put down our first dog. I've always said you shouldn't prolong their life unnecessarily, so when our ten-year-old King Charles spaniel had a stroke, I thought it was time. The vet told me there was an outside chance she'd get better but I looked at her and thought, no. I stuck to my decision and it was awful. She was sitting on my lap and as the injection went in her leg, she looked up at me with her great big eyes and it was too late. I'll never forget that.'

Muffin looks at me a lot these days. How much she can actually see is hard to assess. It's almost an inner vision, a soulful thing. Anyway, she tracks me constantly in my progress through the house. Sometimes the gaze is accusing – 'Isn't it time you fed me/took me out/turned the lights out and went to bed?' – sometimes beseeching – 'Don't go!' – but mostly affectionate and warm.

If she orientates herself primarily through her sense of smell, then she communicates through sight and touch. This is a very tactile dog. The gentler and more prolonged the stroking, the more she likes it, becoming almost feline in her capacity to lengthen, flatten and luxuriate under the warmth of the hand in motion. Lately she lies a little awkwardly: she likes to drop her head lower than her body since having the stroke; she pushes her back legs tightly beneath her. But when the stroking begins, all this changes. She rolls on to her side, lengthens all four legs, stretches her black lips into a little foxy grin and breathes a great big shuddering sigh of contentment. I just trust that the quality of these ordinary moments adds up to, and exceeds, in a lifetime of friendship, the moment that Vincenzi so poignantly describes, when the connection of human to dog, body to body, eye to eye, is finally broken.

September 2011 has been unseasonably warm. The sunlight falls in slanting rays through the trees in the neighbourhood, and the leaves are turning into a shimmer of red and gold, perfectly complementing the tan of Muffin's eyebrows, the feathers of her legs and tail. Every mellow day is a bonus. When we come back from the afternoon walk, Muffin labours up the stairs and lies at the foot of the bed, while I pretend to read and then inevitably drop into a peaceful doze – two silent, slumbering bodies. This is the very essence of our days together: quiet companionship, marked by the breath of life itself.

Psychologist Stanley Coren has written a book about the language of dogs and how they communicate through the movement of their heads, bodies and tails. He works hard to establish some kind of linguistic link, evidence of a separate canine-speak, their own 'doggish' language. For me, the chief joy in my relationship with dogs is the fact that they *cannot* speak. The silence between me and my dog is the ultimate consolation. But the postscript to Coren's book is illuminating. Sleeping beside his dogs, he records the thing that means the most to him: 'It is the sound of dogs breathing . . . As I listen to those soft sounds, I think of some earlier man, lying in a cave or rude shelter, resting on a bed of hides or straw . . . That long ago ancestor also had dogs who lay beside him as he tried to sleep. His dogs breathed these same sounds and these sounds had meaning . . . "I am here with you," the dog's breath said. "We will face this life together."'

As Muffin quietly approaches the end of her life, what I feel most is an enormous sense of privilege that she chose this particular family – one man, one woman, one child – to live alongside and to love. One breath in, little dog, one breath out. It's all we have.

Chapter Two

In the Beginning

S ummer 1999. It was the neat, blonde dog waiting outside the gates of the local primary school that did it. I knew the owner, Maggie, because her son was in the same class as my daughter Molly, and we both came to meet our respective seven-year-olds every day after school. Sandy was a flaxen-haired mongrel, very friendly, very pretty. I was impressed by her demeanour, by the different atmosphere she brought to the otherwise rather brow-beaten group of waiting parents, and, most particularly, I was captivated by her tail. Only a medium-sized dog, Sandy boasted the most spectacular plume at her rear end, arching permanently high and happy, with a cascade of gold and white feathers, which waved beautifully as she walked. Maggie and I used to talk often about dogs and children – domestic talk, but with an undertow of serious intent. The meaning of life lay hidden in these ten-minute consultations, Monday to Friday, at three o'clock outside school.

'Where did you get her?' I asked one day.

'I saw her running in the park. Then, just as we were leaving through the main gates, she came past again. I went up to the woman with her and said, "I've always wanted a dog like that." "Well, you can have her," she replied. Apparently Sandy was a stray. The woman and her friend had been looking after her, hoping she would be reclaimed. But no one had come forward and she was taking her to the dog shelter that day. We said we would have her – and took her home with us right away.'

Like me, Maggie had just one child. The dog, she said, was helpful in this regard. 'It's another being in the house' – another set of lungs, another daily round of cheerful tasks, someone who doesn't answer back. Company. I assumed that Sandy had always looked so well, that the tail had come ready curled and set for sail. Maggie assured me that this was not the case. At first, Sandy's tail had hung sad and low. It is the classic canine barometer, a sure sign of a dog's physical and emotional well-being. One thing was clear: whatever her sad start, Sandy was thriving now; she radiated contentment. All through the summer of 1999, I watched her trotting back and forth to school, stopping gracefully on her way to accept the lumbering pats and strokes of a pack of tiny feral children. The more I saw of her, the more I liked her, and a quiet resolve began to form itself. One day I would have a dog just like Sandy. She would come to school and cheer everyone up, and she, too, would have a billowing flag of triumph for a tail.

*

When Tim first got sick, in the boiling-hot, disastrous summer of 1994, the consultant was clear and brutally honest. 'This cancer can only be contained, never cured. It is a holding operation. *Thymoma*, cancer of the thymus gland, responds well to surgery, but only in the early stages. Your disease is already well established. Chemotherapy is never very effective; radiotherapy sometimes helps.'

These were the only three guns in their arsenal, and they were determined to use them all. So it was, in July 1994, that Tim found himself in a pathetic little cubicle, sectioned off by mere curtain from the next patient receiving devastating news, at the Royal Marsden Hospital in London, being prepared for his first dose of powerful chemicals, all with sinister, Dr Strangelove names: cisplatin, dacarbazine, etoposide. Since his diagnosis had come suddenly, and the nature of the cancer seemed so serious, a plan of action was pressed urgently upon us within days of the initial consultation. As a result, details were ignored in favour of the bigger picture.

'Has anyone explained that this treatment will make you infertile?' asked a kindly male nurse, as he took Tim's blood pressure and checked his temperature. Tim shook his head. It was ten minutes before his first treatment. 'If you would like to store some sperm, we would have to delay the chemotherapy.'

Sometimes decisions are agonising and slow. The mind mulls them over for weeks, even months, before snapping into action. The bigger the decision, the slower the process can be. Tim had just ten minutes to decide whether he would be a father again.

Meanwhile, he was psyched, as he had never been psyched before, to undergo a process more gruelling than any in his life so far. To delay this procedure any longer than necessary would be torture – for both of us. We looked at each other and decided on the spot. No. Proceed. There would be no more children.

It seems an arbitrary way to decide things, but the pressure of that Sword of Damocles, glinting overhead, clarified the mind beautifully. And somehow I had always known that I would have only one child. That this child would lose her father so young seemed mean, unfair and sad. That she would have no siblings just seemed natural and inevitable. She can fight me about that when she chooses, but she shows no sign of doing so, so far. But what now becomes clear to me is that my longing for a dog, five years after that wretched little scene was played out in that London hospital, was not just about the animal. The arrival of Muffin filled a gap in all our lives. For Molly, she was a funny, furry sibling. For Tim, she was a playful distraction. For me, she was many things, ever changing, ever delightful. One of those things, although I would never have recognised the fact, was a replacement baby; a baby, moreover, who – unlike Molly, unlike any human offspring – would never grow up.

One of my favourite children's stories is J. M. Barrie's *Peter Pan* – not so much for the crocodile and the pirate and the endless derring-do; more for the character of Peter himself and the magic he brings. Who exactly is this androgynous, ethereal character, leaping from moonbeam to moonbeam in his pointy slippers, luring all the children away from their earthly moorings? I thought I knew. I was born of the David Bowie generation – that crop-haired, boy–girl cohort of dungaree-wearing screamers, who steadfastly refused to grow up, but then, all of a sudden, found themselves fifty years old and weighed down by the gravity of life. I identified with Peter, and the grief on the other side of his rainbow, absolutely.

The best stage production of *Peter Pan* I have ever seen was by the Royal Shakespeare Company in London in 1983, with the effervescent and miraculous Mark Rylance as Peter. This Peter – skinny, fleet of foot, ready to fly and eager to fight – was brim-full of mischief and energy. He was everybody's antidote to life's mundane little dullnesses. He was adventure itself. I was still young and single at the time, so I borrowed a friend's little girl to go and watch the show. When the piece was over, we both stood as close to the stage as we possibly could and gazed at the dark empty space. Neither of us could bear to leave. We were the very last two in the auditorium: one of us tall and thin, the other one tiny and trim. And both of us had stardust in our hair.

When Muffin came charging into my life, sixteen years later, there was more than a hint of Pan in her demeanour. She was dashing and reckless and absolutely overflowing with *joie de vivre*, feathers in her ears, a waggish red handkerchief round her neck. She seemed ageless and hopeful and full of good humour. Every time I watched her run through woods and over grassy Yorkshire hills, she seemed to embody Peter's words in a flowing stream of action: 'I'll teach you to ride on the wind's back, and away we go ... Second star to the right and straight on till morning.' Even now, when she is slow with arthritis, her face misty with age, she has a certain glint in her eye. She has grown old, but she has never grown up. Dogs, unlike other animals, continue to play long into their adult life. They like a good time. It's why we need them so badly: to shake the thoughts out of our heads, and the oppressive weight of adult responsibilities out of our hearts.

Maggie's dog came to her unbidden. She literally bumped into her in the local park. For us, the search took a little longer, and was a little more contrived. But the way things turned out, like Sandy, Muffin seemed to find us, quite as much as we chose her.

Money was always tight in our house. Tim's work as an Arts Administrator was affected by his illness, with time off for treatment, and the after-effects of surgery and the endless deadening drugs. My work, always sporadic as a freelance writer and T'ai Chi teacher, was in turn affected by Tim. It was a constant game of dominoes. But, in December 1999, I wrote an article for the local paper and received the princely fee of £80 for my trouble. This was exactly what it cost to buy a rescue dog from the RSPCA – I had checked.

We decided to pay a visit to the local dog shelter, now closed down – stray dogs, it seems, are one of the first victims in a recession. The building was huge and daunting. It lurked amidst a collection of industrial warehouses on Kirkstall Road, outside Leeds city centre. The area was bleak, Dickensian. The building was grey, cold, concrete. From the outside, the distant sound of dogs howling filtered through. We had visions of a harrowing walk past endless rows of dogs behind bars, each one beseeching us to be chosen, but the RSPCA were better organised than that. We were ushered in to a waiting room and given a folder full of the current inmates. Each page ran a hilarious mugshot of the dog, accompanied by a short write-up of its history, temperament and the kind of household it would be best suited to.

Several of the dogs we were drawn to were ruled out immediately by the stern invocations of the write-up: 'Not suitable for children!', 'Better in a child-free household!' In amongst the pack were a brother and sister mongrel combination: 'Bud', a light chestnut male, and 'Sonia', a black-haired spaniel–collie cross. 'Sonia' was later to be our Muffin. Bud was deemed too aggressive for our nervous daughter, so we left him off our shortlist. We ended up with three candidates: Candy, Barnaby and Sonia. Rather than have us go to the cages, a handler brought the dogs to us, one at a time. It was hard to know who was the more anxious, the candidates or the potential owners. It was a stifling, nerve-racking process.

First out of the door was Candy. She was big, blonde, boisterous – and decidedly smelly. Molly shrank behind a chair as she came bounding up. In a classroom situation, my daughter was always quiet (sometimes subversive, but always in a whisper, never a shout). In a class the people she avoided with horror were those with a loud laugh, a heavy step and a cheerful disregard for personal space. If Candy had been a human, she would have been the noisy joker bursting bubble gum on the back row. Almost the second we saw her, good-looking girl as she undoubtedly was, we knew that Candy was not the one.

Second up was Barnaby, a tousle-haired, floppy-eared fellow, with spaghetti limbs and an enthusiastic grin. Barnaby was a party animal all right. 'Needs plenty of exercise,' said his write-up. 'Not ideal around small children. Tends towards excitability.' I liked this fellow. He was handsome and keen, but we worried that he might get bored. Racing around on a farm would be more his thing than a quiet, semi-detached existence on a surburban estate.

Sonia was the last of our choices. She was also the smallest – and in the worst condition by far. She came darting nervously into the room, with a highly strung, almost desperate air. It was clear that she was suffering. The handler said she cried incessantly in the cages, and could not bear to be shut in. But there was also something determined in her gait – a little streak of iron running through her thin, pathetic frame.

What followed next was strange. The other two dogs had run indiscriminately through the room. They barely registered us as individuals, but just went where they were led in a haphazard, oblivious way – not Sonia. She ran straight for Tim. He was the one she chose, bounding to him with a determined spring and making a massive, messy fuss of him, all teeth, tongue and saliva. He was astonished, and flattered, I think, that the little dog had chosen him. She was a shambolic little individual with bad skin and dreadful teeth; she was emaciated and malnourished; and, worst of all, her thin string of a tail hung down, limp and lifeless, between her hind legs. Both Tim and Molly said they liked her the best, but I was less than impressed.

Several days went by. Tim and I had agreed to let the matter rest for a while, but it was difficult to get those dogs out of my head. Why had both husband and daughter fallen for Sonia and I hadn't? Why had the little dog made such a beeline for Tim, as if he were her prize and she wasn't going to leave this world without owning him? What hidden canine charms had I missed? My mind wouldn't let it go. In the end, I decided to visit her again, on my own, and find out about Sonia for myself.

I made an appointment to take her for a trial walk. This was a Bank of Switzerland gold safe procedure. I had to hand over my passport and bank card to ensure I did not abscond with the dog under my coat. Then Sonia was brought out, like a high-security prisoner, fastened to a double lead. 'She's a bit dizzy,' they explained. 'This will give you more control.' They weren't kidding. This was one bonkers little dog. One sniff of the outside wintry air and she was off like a whirling dervish, running in every direction at once, as if desperate to escape from everything, including herself. We were on a busy main road, with not a tree in sight. The dog's lead discipline was non-existent, and she was tying me in knots. She was busy, but, like an automaton, oblivious to the world around her. This mission seemed doomed to failure.

Further up the road was a small piece of scrubland. I had been advised to head for that, but to keep Sonia on a tight lead throughout. At last, there were a couple of trees, a hint of grass. As we passed the trees, a sudden gust of wind whipped up behind us, sending us both into a scamper and loosening a few brown leaves from the lower branches. Sonia seemed to come alive in an instant. She saw a leaf drifting past her nose and gave chase. Round in tight little circles she ran, determined to bag her dead leaf, completely caught up in the fun, the thrill of the chase. I watched her play, and saw what looked suspiciously like a grin stretch stealthily across her chops. I realised this dog had a *sense of humour*. Underneath all her neuroses, her multiple physical woes, Sonia had a spark of life. It was all I needed to convince me: this little dog should definitely come home with us. She was the one.

A few years ago some friends of mine decided to adopt a child. The procedure was lengthy and daunting: essays were written by all family members; physical and psychological checks were carried out. The invasiveness was brutal, relentless. It was hard to know whether to be impressed at the thoroughness of the government agencies or appalled at their sledgehammer tactics. Adopting a dog is nothing like as rigorous, but I was still surprised by the demands that were made.

Once we had put in an official bid for the dog (and I had made my peace with the family for my secret visit), we had to fill in a plethora of forms. After that there was an official home visit – and questions, questions, questions. Was the garden secure? Where would the dog sleep? Was someone at home during the day to walk her and keep her company? Did we have any experience of living with dogs? Did we have any idea what we were taking on? At the end of the visit, I was sure we would be turned down, and almost wished we would be; I felt so deflated. Luckily, I was wrong, and Sonia, sad little ratbag of a creature that she then was, was released, ready spayed and microchipped, into our tender care. Life would never be the same again.

In a recent *Guardian* newspaper article, Gavin Newsham wrote about the havoc caused by the adorable little labradoodle puppy, new to his household. 'Whatever it is that has brought us to this point, it's difficult to argue that the impact of the dog's arrival in our house has been nothing short of seismic. A recent survey by Esure found that a pet dog will cause around 2,000 arguments between families during the dog's average lifespan of 12.8 years. We've certainly had our share already. Everything from whose turn it is to walk the thing (mine, usually) to whose bright idea it was to get one in the first place (not mine, never), the very presence of a dog in one's home is, to me at least, little more than a joyless series of flashpoints to be circumnavigated until those 12.8 years are up.'

Oh dear. It's a good thing I didn't read this before tripping off gaily to the dog shelter all those years ago. It's also fortunate that I didn't realise quite how long-lived and tenacious our own dog would turn out to be.

The RSPCA don't say a great deal about the background of the dogs in their care. Considering the horrible cruelty and neglect they come across, their discretion is remarkable. Sonia's provenance, therefore, remains largely a mystery. We know she was from South Leeds, because rehoming is always to a different part of the city, and we live in the North. We also know that she was one of a large collection of dogs allowed to breed and run amok in a high-rise flat. Her estimated age was three and she had never been allowed out until rescued by the RSPCA. (The neighbours tipped them off.) She was half-starved and almost feral. No violence was suspected, but she always flinches when a hand comes near the top of her head, so I believe she got slapped a few times. She was also very timid with men in the beginning – probably because she received those slaps from a man – which makes her instant adherence to Tim all the more remarkable. It's hard to imagine the filth in a flat where the dogs are never let out, hard to imagine the pain of a hunger that is never satisfied – either for affection or food.

Rescue dogs are overwhelmingly grateful to their rescuers – it's what makes them such satisfying pets. The sense of neglect and abandonment they feel is lifelong and acute. Biologist John Bradshaw researched the behaviour of rescue dogs and noted the speed of attachment to a new owner. '... Just a few minutes of friendly attention from one person on two consecutive days is enough to make some of these unowned dogs desperate to stay with that person; when left on their own, these dogs will howl, scratch at the door that the person has left through, or jump up at the window to see where she has gone.'

The separation anxiety that Muffin experiences has crippled many attempts at a lengthy holiday away. The sense of guilt I feel when leaving her, even for a few hours, is profound. 'Wait till your daughter leaves home,' people said. 'What freedom you'll feel!' Oh really? Molly has been independent for years. It is Muffin who remains the mute and loving millstone around my neck. Not content to have me in the same house, Muffin needs me in the same room, wherever possible. Even at her advanced age, she manages to stumble up the stairs and hover, wheezing, on the landing, trying to work out which room I am in – bedroom, bathroom, toilet, study – before galumphing back down to her basket again – just checking.

The first few weeks with a new dog are always chaos, but training a messed-up rescue dog is every shade of madness. The easiest part was renaming her. 'Sonia' was ridiculously girly. Muffin – double chocolate chip, due to her black and tan colouring and Galaxy brown eyes – was an obvious and cheerful choice. Muffin herself was far from cheerful: she was disorientated and anxious. She didn't know day from night. She pooed and peed indiscriminately, whenever she felt like it. She refused to eat the complete dry food the vet had recommended. She had no idea at all what her basket was for. She hardly slept, and panted and barked with shock whenever anyone came to the door – or when she was left alone behind one.

It felt as if we were on 24-hour watch, and none of us had much of a clue how to make things better. For the first few nights, Tim and I took it in turns to sleep on the sofa in the front room with the dog. She wandered about in the dark all night, barging into furniture and whining softly. I suspect she had never learned to sleep properly at all, living, as she had done, in a rough old pack of dogs, constantly having to watch her back. By the look of her when we found her, she must surely have qualified as the runt of the litter, and therefore the one who took all the blows and none of the food. She was so tired, so wired, so hungry. But slowly, slowly, she settled.

After a while, we introduced the notion of her own bed. She looked at it and refused to get in – like a baby with a new cot. Finally, Molly decided to climb in herself, and Muffin immediately snuggled in beside her. 'Well, why didn't you just say?' was the look in her eye. I chucked the fancy dry food away after the first week and bought the cheapest tin of dog food I could find. She wolfed it down in seconds. Now we were making progress.

Always eager to learn, I had borrowed an armful of library books on dog training. Following our instincts would have been a safer bet, but I made the mistake of playing it by the book. Echoing the brittle tones of those 1950s baby-care manuals, where baby was wheeled to the bottom of the garden in its pram and left to cry alone, the books I read suggested firmly that we shut the dog in the kitchen for short periods of time to get her used to being alone. The result was cataclysmic. Muffin wailed and barked and scratched her paws raw. The barrier between her and us was simply unbearable to her. We quickly learned that this dog, who had, after all, been incarcerated her entire life, needed an eye on every exit, and a sense of connection to her adoptive family, at all times. We put her bed in the hall at the bottom of the stairs and kept all doors open, and she gradually became calm and comfortable.

Molly was patient with the new dog, but she was jealous too. Up till now she had been the centre of attention; now both parents were permanently distracted and desperate to appease the new arrival.

'You love her more than me, don't you?' she asked, accusingly.

'No,' I replied. 'But she's a damn sight more work, that's for sure.'

It didn't help that Muffin – uncannily like a human child – realised early on that Molly's room was by far the most interesting in the house. It was stuffed full of TOYS! Every so often, Muffin would sneak upstairs and steal a little something to take back to her basket and chew to bits. Puppies and young dogs are notorious for their unwitting destructiveness. They will cut and sharpen their teeth on just about any available object, from the morning post to the legs of your best sofa. Muffin was quite restrained in this regard. But it was nearly the end between her and Molly when she stole a tiny plastic dog from Molly's Barbie collection, took it down to her basket, chewed off the corner of its ear, then buried it under her blanket to hide the evidence. She obviously recognised a fellow canine, though the difference between a poodle parlour Barbie accessory and our little string lug of a mongrel could hardly have been greater.

One of the most difficult issues we faced in the first weeks with this crazy, half-feral dog was toilet training. Something tells me that her former feckless owners were unlikely to have installed canine litter boxes. Muffin had never been let out in her life, so for her anywhere and everywhere would do. Dog poo is disgusting, wherever you find it. When you tread in it, barefoot, first thing in the morning, at the top of the stairs, on your way to the bathroom, it feels like nothing less than a personal assault.

Rescue dogs often mark their territory this way. The RSPCA carefully omitted this piece of information. It was a veteran dog walker in our local wood who confided that his rescue dog – otherwise beautifully behaved – regularly left a steaming pile outside the closed bedroom door at night. Whether this behaviour is to keep the hapless owner under control – to show that the dog is boss – I have never been able to figure out. It is just unfortunate that it was the ultra-fastidious Tim who landed his heel in dog mess only one week after Muffin's arrival.

'Muffin!' he bellowed, outraged, from the top of the stairs.

The dog, in reply, cowered at the bottom of the stairs, terror-stricken and frozen solid, as the monster man bore down on her. I had to intervene. It is almost impossible not to take it personally when the pet uses your home as a toilet, and it certainly took a while for them to become friends after that.

*

As Muffin reaches the end of her life, she increasingly comes to resemble the creature she was at the very beginning. Her frame is thin and wasting. The tail has gone back between her legs, stringy and rather sad. She is less sure of the rhythm of her days. Sometimes she stands in the middle of a room, disorientated and alone. There is a fog in her eyes where there used to be starshine. Worst of all, her toilet habits have regressed to those early days. She was, for years, an obliging and reliable dog. She was walked twice a day, and she pooed twice a day – never on the pavement, never underfoot and never in the garden, which was definitely out of bounds. The rules have been relaxed now. In the past few weeks even the short trot to the woods would outdo her. I have got used to trailing around after her, among the herbaceous borders, plastic bag in hand.

When I first started gardening, I used to have nightmares about slugs: it was not the glory of the shrubs and flowers I planted, but the vileness of the slimy pests who chewed them to bits, that rose to the surface of my mind in sleep. In the same way, when I wake up every morning, I don't gaze down fondly, as I used to, at the little furball in her basket, positioned still at the bottom of the stairs; now my eyes dart nervously to the hallway beyond her. Has she made it through the night, or is there a pile of muck to be negotiated and sanitised before my morning cup of tea? I have started getting up earlier and earlier to beat the dog clock. It doesn't really work. She is quite random.

New, young dogs are very hard work, but they settle down.

Old dogs demand so much more. I find it impossible to believe that I have grown older – Peter Pan glows, like a flint, in my heart – and it is simply incomprehensible that our funny, wild little dog is, by comparison, much older still. My patience refuses me too often. 'You wouldn't expect a ninety-year-old to walk so fast, would you?' a friend rebuked me recently. There are no Zimmer frames or wheelchairs for animals, but a measure of quiet respect is the least I can offer.

In the first year of her life with us, the issue we faced with Muffin was not how to get her going, but how on earth to slow her down. The vet had told us she had a heart murmur. This, you might have thought, would make her breathless and slow her progress. The opposite seemed to be the case. Tim was still well enough to work at this stage, and my job was based at home, so walking the dog was initially my domain. It was less of a chore, more a daily adventure.

Although she was painfully malnourished when we got her, Muffin put on weight with speed and efficiency. It was only a few weeks until she, too, had a tail of splendour – black on top, fringed white and tan below – to match Sandy's. Her eyes, dull and glazed to start with, gradually took on a shine and humour. She got stronger by the day. She had verve. It was time for the serious dog walking to begin.

Once again, I put my nose into the manuals for advice. One thing was clear: she could not be let off the lead for some time. Whenever we left the house, she took life with a run, skip and jump. The outside world was chock full of wonder to her, and

I started to regard my surroundings with a different eye accordingly. A new baby makes everything precious and washed clean; a new dog makes the most boring tuft of grass – the most familiar route to and from school – nothing short of miraculous.

Muffin was delighted with everything and everyone she encountered. I started her quietly. There was a little patch of open ground behind our house, with a hint of a hill, surrounded by hedges and a few old trees, called, somewhat euphemistically, Fairy Woods. (Judging by the groups of dubious-looking youths who gathered there at sunset, Dealers' Dell might have been a more accurate title, but at least they were discreet.) At first, our walks were just there and back, several times a day. Then we progressed to the local wood.

I decided some kind of proper training was in order, inside – 'Sit', 'Stay', from one end of the hall to the other – then out. Muffin was a greedy dog and quick to learn. The lure of a doggy chocolate drop clinched the deal and she started to respond to command, and to listen to the tone of my voice, as well as the content. No one else in the house did, so that was a pleasing change. Sooner or later, I knew it had to happen: she would have to go off the lead outside, and I needed to trust that she would come back to me when I called. The first time I set her free is in my memory still, indelibly etched. If there were music to describe it, it would have to be Beethoven's 'Ode to Joy'.

We went to Fairy Woods; as a small, contained space, it was ideal. I walked her to the top of the hill. As usual, she was straining at the collar, running and sniffing and turning her head this way and that. So much to see! So much to do! Then I stopped still, leaned down and unclipped the lead. There was a split second where she registered what was happening – and then she was off. Released from the constraints of the lead, she could follow her instincts entirely. Being part collie, her main instinct was to run, fast and hard and gleeful, in ever-increasing circles, round and round and round. It made me dizzy, just to watch her. Ears flying, tongue lolling, tail waving high, the biggest doggy grin you ever saw plastered across her daft little face. It was a privilege to be a witness to this. She was a pretty little songbird set free from a tiny cage and floating up into the bluest, widest sky imaginable. There was nothing I could do – or wanted to do – to stop her. In the end, she just ran out of steam, and came back to me at the centre of the circle, paws flailing, tongue ragged, saliva slopped across her muzzle, and was still.

I really should have thrown those dog manuals away at this point, but where else could I get advice? All our friends were cat lovers. The nearest dog-training class was three miles away on a Sunday morning, and we had no car. To this day I don't know if I was right, but I did it by the book, and it worked like a charm.

'When you first let your dog off the lead, you have to be sure it comes back to you. One way to do that is to hide. Slip out of sight behind a tree and make the dog come and look for you – a reversal of the usual order of things. Keep doing this at regular intervals and the dog will have to track you all the time. It won't dare disappear, because you did it first.'

Ludicrous as I looked, stupid as I felt, I put this strange theory into practice. On all our early jaunts to the wood, I would sidle behind trees, suddenly change direction and head off at a tangent, trusting that Muffin would instinctively seek me out and stay close by. I may have looked like some weird female flasher, but it did the trick. Muffin was constantly alert to my movements. She searched and followed me resolutely, never once, even in the middle of the most absorbing scent trail, forgetting to keep me on her radar.

'That poor dog,' said a psychotherapist friend, 'you have made her totally neurotic.' Maybe she was right – anxiety over separation was always high in Muffin's repertoire of emotional tics – but, in all the years we have had her, she has never once (until well into her dotage) got lost, run away or refused to return to her owners. Her nerves may be in shreds, although I doubt it, looking at her, but mine have been saved by this one simple trick: forget the treats and rewards, just disappear on a regular basis. It is not what the dog expects, and its first instinct will be to come and find.

I only ever let Muffin off the lead away from roads. I was always envious of those owners who had their dogs trotting neatly to heel down busy city streets, but I was under no illusions. Muffin obeyed the 'Come here!' rule, but *staying* here was always a problem. She was easy to distract: sensory deprivation as a puppy meant that the outside world of random noises, sights and smells would always overwhelm her to a certain degree. Besides, she was a chaser: cats, squirrels, birds, plastic bags, empty crisp packets – whatever veered into view and was smaller than her was fair game. Sometimes she just chased shadows and dreams.

She slipped the lead only once, just outside our house. It was very early days still, and she went crazy. She ran backwards and forwards, across the road, into neighbours' gardens, behind parked cars, in an ecstasy of naughtiness.

'You'll never get her back now,' said the next-door neighbour, watching the dog's erratic behaviour with appalled fascination.

'I will,' I said, and I just waited. The faster she ran, the more still I became. I sank down into a crouch and quietly called her. Hysteria cranked her up; she liked the meditative approach – this dog would have been best buddies with the Buddha. It took a long, long time, but in the end she stopped in her tracks and walked back to me and sat down at my feet. We were lucky that day. If a car had driven past, she would have been under the wheels, no question, but the road remained clear. I did get a new lead, nonetheless, and held on to her a bit more tightly, just in case.

A few weeks after Muffin's arrival, the inspector came to see how she was getting on. My mother used to be in the Ladies' Fellowship, a sort of rival gang to the Women's Institute. They were a stalwart bunch of women, organised, intelligent and forthright. Occasionally, I came into the hall where they met to drop off some refreshments, or deliver some sort of visual aid for the talk of the day. I never lingered – those ladies terrified me. Our home visitor was made of similar stock. She was sturdy, sensibly dressed, with a no-nonsense handshake. She quizzed us thoroughly about Muffin's progress, examined the dog, and watched how she behaved with a sharp and gimlet eye. At that stage, Muffin was firmly attached to me, so she lay under my legs the whole time, peering out at the stranger occasionally with a wary gaze. I think she was as intimidated as we were. After a full hour, our inquisitor finally snapped her notebook shut and stood up to leave. She paused at the door, ignoring the humans in the room, looked directly at Muffin and said, 'I hope you have a long and happy life.' Muffin was now officially adopted. It was just before Christmas 1999. This was one present, live and kicking, who would not be going back.

New Year's Eve that year was a big one. Never one to get excited by 31 December celebrations, even I was forced to do something for the millennium. We had friends round in the evening, and they persuaded us to join them at a party later on. The party was in a field on the edge of the city – huge bonfire, fireworks to follow. We didn't like leaving the dog at home alone, so, reluctantly, we took her with us. Tim wasn't feeling very well. Occasionally, the cancer drugs made him nauseous. I should have read the signs and kept us all at home. Even my daughter, thrilled to be allowed to stay up past midnight, was nervous about the fireworks.

The juvenile period for dogs, from three months to one year, is a critical time in their development. The early sensitivity and attachment to mother is gone, and puppies are curious to learn about the world around them. Ideally, to make your dog properly 'bombproof', you need to introduce them to a wide range of stimuli during this period, carefully acclimatising them to the relentlessly social – and sometimes astonishingly loud – world of human beings. Muffin, cooped up in her filthy high-rise, had none of this early education, thus she got sick every time she travelled in a car, growled at every newcomer to cross the threshold, and was utterly, irredeemably terrified of thunderstorms, sudden loud bangs – and fireworks. She was a prime candidate for noise phobia from the start, but we had no idea. And trouble – big trouble – was just around the corner.

The weather that New Year's Eve was crisp and clear – no wind, no rain. Every sound carried for miles. The field was full of people. The fire burned brightly. The night closed in around its red heart, black as pitch. As midnight approached, we gathered in a circle to sing and to wish the world well. There were some poems, some gentle reflection. Then the clock struck twelve and all hell broke loose. Not only did the field's fireworks go off with a bang – incredibly loud and incredibly close – but hilltop fireworks for miles and miles around us hit the inky skies. The heavens were ablaze with flashes of light and sound. It felt like the Tudor age all over again, with Elizabeth I, glittering with jewels, sailing her barge down the Thames in a triumphant procession of opulence and excess: a fire burning in every port, an ox slain in village and town, beer and wine consumed by the gallon. A sort of bacchanalian madness.

We were like spectres at the feast. My daughter, who had already freaked out when offered a simple sparkler, was cowering in a corner; Tim was throwing up in a ditch (disease, not booze, the unfortunate cause); and the dog was in an absolute ecstasy of hyperactive terror. From that day onwards, Firework Night became a date in the calendar permanently ringed round in warning black marker pen. Taking Muffin to that party was the worst possible thing we could ever have done. I felt like ringing the RSPCA welfare visitor and confessing: 'Take my dog back. I am obviously unfit to have her. And while you are at it, you'd better take my daughter and my husband too. I haven't got a clue what I am doing. Help!'

Inevitably, things settled down. All the pieces of our small family unit had been thrown high in the air. When they finally landed, some time in the new year of 2000, they formed a new pattern – a more solid and substantial square to the previous triangle. Muffin, scatty little canine trickster that she was, had done just what I had hoped. She provided diversion and comfort – an extra dimension, non-verbal, animal, sensitively tuned – to bolster us all up. Once the finer details of training and the hair-raising antics around dog walking were settled and sorted, we were able to enjoy in Muffin what every good dog should bring to the household: her companionship and unconditional affection, her irrepressible sense of fun.

These days, Muffin has no time for her old toys – Hippo, Tuggy Toy, Wayne the soft-bellied reindeer with the golden antlers; after all, there is sleeping to be done. But as a young dog, Muffin's appetite for play was insatiable. The minute she heard the key turning in the lock, she was up and running. She always gave a most joyous 'hello' – panting and jumping in excitement, tail waving madly, brown eyes aglow. Then she would dash to her basket and pick out some mangy, stinky old toy and carry it through to the front room, bearing her trophy proudly aloft and daring us to snatch it from her, which is when the fun began.

Tuggy Toy, a thick length of brightly coloured knotted rope, was best of all. Human at one end, defiant dog at the other, the tug-of-war could go on indefinitely. Exceptionally strong, both in her teeth and hindquarters, Muffin was a sight to behold. Mouth stuffed with rope, bum in the air, a low playful growl emitting from her tightly clamped jaw, rising in pitch as her adversary increased the pressure, then settling back into her throat with a smoky, jazz singer's absorption as she gained the upper hand – this was one contented dog. This was the sound of happiness.

I was never a sporty girl. I grew too quickly; I was tall and lanky, long before puberty, and painfully shy. Even at my small primary school, whose main cohort of pupils came from the local housing estate, and were underfed and shabbily dressed, I was never first choice for netball and rounders teams. Even in that motley bunch, I was deemed wanting. But everyone gets their moment of glory, and I had two.

In the final year before secondary school, I hit a brief but joyful peak in the high jump, using the scissors technique, landing on thin sand, the old-fashioned way. In the year before that, I discovered a talent for catching the ball. Throwing it back was always a problem – I didn't have much power in my shoulders and upper arms – but my hand–eye coordination was spot on. By some miracle, I was chosen as third post for the school rounders team. The bowler was Tina Sandford, a fast and nimble player, and between us we made a swift and deadly combination. She would bowl, the player would strike, I would catch the ball and lunge for the post just in time to get the runner out, then deal the ball back to Tina, ready for the next sucker. It felt powerful – and fun. I can still remember the smack of the ball as it landed cleanly in my hands, the sense of satisfaction in a job well done.

Muffin would have made a great third post. Her ability to catch a ball, the balance and poise of her body as she launched herself into the air, all four paws aloft, ears flying, eyes and mouth spread wide to see and receive, was breathtaking – like a canine Nijinsky in full flight. The ball was probably her favourite of all the toys, and it was Tim who honed her skills when he took over dog walking full time.

As 2000 progressed, it became clear that the commute to work, followed by a full and demanding day at the office, was just too much for Tim to manage. Six years into the cycle of his disease, having survived major chest surgery, several punishing rounds of chemotherapy and all the radiotherapy his body could bear, he was still doing well, still on his feet, but he was tired.

Something had to change. Angels, or at least benevolent spirits – truly evolved human beings – come into our lives when we are at our lowest ebb. Plenty of 'angels' flitted into Tim's life when he most needed them.

His boss certainly qualified for honorary wings. Duncan fought for Tim, from the moment he heard of his illness, with all the weapons in his armoury. He arranged for Tim to work from home. He changed his job description. He investigated sickness pay and special benefits. He went out of his way to make Tim's life as comfortable and connected as it could be, for as long as was humanly possible. I cannot thank him enough for the kindness he showed.

The one failing he had was an unfortunate one: HE DID NOT LIKE DOGS. Home visits, which he made frequently, with wine and fruit and all manner of goodies, were a little taxing in that regard. Muffin, with the unerring instinct that dogs have, was determined to win him over. She would make a bee-line for him – the horror on his face was a picture – and never left him alone for the entire length of his stay. In the end, she had to be consigned to her basket in the hall. She was not pleased. The two of them were never reconciled. Duncan is the only person, out of hundreds of visitors through the years, who remained stalwartly impervious to the dog's charms – the one that got away.

Duncan aside, Muffin was a convenient buffer whenever tensions ran high in the household. None of us were shouty people. Our first line of attack, man, woman and child, was silent sulking. 'There is nothing more noisy than your silences,' a friend once remarked. Although she could deliver a killer glare when the occasion demanded it, Muffin had no notion of bad temper at all, no investment in punitive atmospheres or mind games of any sort. She was just a happy little dog.

She was worth thousands of pounds in therapy, with her simple demands and bountiful generosity. How can you stay sad when there is a dog to be walked, or when that same dog is bouncing up and down beside you, simply begging you to play ball, just one more time? Animals put us to shame with their simplicity, their gratitude, their absolute ignorance of blame and self-pity. When we were lost in our individual bubbles of isolation, as Tim succumbed to the rigours of his illness, Muffin would appear and demand to be tickled (just under her armpits for preference – or maybe a good rub of the belly instead?). She knew if someone was sad: she lay at their feet in sympathy. She had uncanny radar, seeking out the person in need and laying a warm head on his or her lap.

What is it that dogs do for us? Why do we need them so much? Animals are connected, powerfully, to the rhythms of nature. What they lack in intellect, they make up in instinct. Through the years, I have been impressed with Muffin's easy acceptance of life. Whatever the weather, the season, the mood or expectations of her human family, she has been willing to go along with it all. She can ebb and flow like the tide. Nothing fazes her. It would be hard to prove that an animal has a spirit, or a soul, although I see it every time I look in Muffin's eyes. But it is impossible to deny animals' absolute surrender to the moment. To dissemble is beyond them. They are present, right *here,* right *now.* What else is there?

Molly and Muffin were the shining jewels in our family. Each of them – young child, young dog – offered in abundance something that had been curiously compromised since Tim and I had been together: the sense of a new beginning.

Although it never felt like it, being a fretful sort of individual, I must have had a very sheltered upbringing. There was no divorce, no illness, no accident and no death in our household throughout the whole of my childhood. Relatives died, but we children were, in the custom of the time, kept well away from the evidence.

The first funeral I went to was that of my beloved grandmother; I was thirty years old. I would have been happy to wait another thirty years for the next one, since the whole thing unnerved me completely. If the Victorians made a fetish of death, then the modern Elizabethans have subscribed wholesale to its taboo. When our cat died in a traffic accident, when I was eight years old, and I demanded to see the body, my father found my request both alarming and macabre. (I now realise it was healthy psychologically – seeing the evidence of death with my own eyes helped me come to terms with the reality.) Then, when our family dog died, there was the briefest of phone calls between me and my parents, a brisk imparting of information, and a strong desire on both sides to avoid the obvious distress lurking under the surface of the conversation. We were, as a family, for all our noise and bluster, alarmingly skilled at sweeping the dirty stuff swiftly under the carpet.

Grandmother's funeral, as it turned out, was the start of a long series of losses. This was 1987: the AIDS era. I had many gay friends in London, and my best friend had found out he was HIV positive. He was just one of several in my close circle who got sick very quickly. It was a horrible time. Treatment was random and ineffectual back then. Prejudice was rampant. The stigma these men faced was like something from the Middle Ages. Soon, the endless dreary rounds of isolation wards began. What I remember most vividly is the smell of rotting fruit and sad, decaying flowers on dismal hospital windowsills. I remember, too, the panic of the phone calls in the middle of the night, asking me to go and sit by someone's bedside, as they gasped and struggled their way through bouts of pneumonia, and succumbed to cancers, skin diseases, wild fevers and bone-shattering chills. Funerals for young, vibrant, talented men became commonplace during that time of my life. And though they were magnificent occasions, transforming the way the British mourn their dead for ever, it was, to a whole generation, an utter devastation.

Inevitably, my dear friend died too. I had loved him for eighteen years. We met when we were students: we grew up together. He made me laugh more than anyone else before or since. Although it is twenty years since he died – a longer time with him gone than we shared when he was alive – I miss him every day. It is a measure of the enduring taboo around this disease that I still cannot write his real name for fear of upsetting people. Let's call him John.

John had a little dog, too. A jaunty mongrel, who doted on his owner and brought a lot of happiness – and enforced exercise – to a stricken group of people. On the day of John's funeral, there was a celebration at the London Lighthouse (an oasis for AIDS sufferers at that time). As the ceremony came to a close, the coffin was carried out to music and wild applause, a standing ovation. As the procession exited through the doors, John's dog, who had sat quietly throughout the morning, made a sudden lunge at his lead to get to the coffin. He was determined to follow his master in death, as in life. How on earth did he know John was inside that wooden box? We underestimate these dogs at our great cost.

Tim and I met in 1989. It was a hot summer and all I remember from our first few heady encounters was a tall man with a radiant smile and an enormous capacity for staying up late – and for drink. We walked for miles that summer, through Regent's Park and up Primrose Hill, where he lived, throughout the day. We ate and drank and talked for hours through the night. It was a happy awakening, a calm time.

And yet illness was in the picture, right from the start. John was already very sick and I was involved in his care. Tim, too, was getting mysterious symptoms in his left shoulder. He would sweat with the pain of it at night, tossing and turning for hours on end. One evening, on Hampstead Heath, he had to let me down from a piggyback ride suddenly, because his shoulder was hurting badly. With an extraordinary, yet characteristic, Yorkshire stoicism, he chose to ignore these significant pains. He assumed he had strained a muscle gardening for a friend and blithely carried on regardless. By autumn 1993, things had progressed. He kept getting flu-like illnesses. He was debilitated and exhausted all the time.

We had a young child by then – Molly was just one year old. She had been a source of huge pleasure and delight from the moment she appeared. Some babies come brand new into the world; others seem to arrive already wise and knowing. Molly, with her dark, clear gaze and serene beauty, was one of the wise ones. She was a quiet soul, never unduly demanding – a beacon of hope in difficult circumstances – but babies need lots of care, whatever their temperament. When Tim started to feel ill, I, too, was struggling – with the cares of new motherhood and simple tiredness. John had died earlier that year, so grief had already come to call.

In April 1994, one year to the day after John's death, Tim received his cancer diagnosis. The cancer was relentless in its progress. There were periods of remission – breathing spaces, moments of grace – followed by an acceleration in the disease. Crisis after calm, over and over again. Following his initial diagnosis and surgery in summer 1994, there was a two-year lull in the illness's activity. Our life in London had become strained beyond endurance by poor living conditions – a psychotic neighbour, followed by a move to a sink estate, dominated by drug dealing and vandalism – and troubles with work. We decided to move north to Leeds, Tim's home city, and make a new start for ourselves. In a mood of classic denial, I think we both believed that by moving away from London we could leave the illness behind us too.

We arrived in Leeds in August 1996. By October, scans showed that Tim's cancer was active again. We began a familiar trawl of hospitals, clinics and GPs' waiting rooms. So much for our new beginning. By 1999, Tim's rare and intransigent disease had finally defeated a whole phalanx of highly trained doctors and sophisticated treatment options. He received his terminal diagnosis with characteristic courage and quiet despair. There would be no more fresh starts. It was now a matter of waiting for the inevitable to happen.

Into this atmosphere of underlying tension and strain bounced one small and lively dog. Who cared that Tim had cancer? He could throw a ball, couldn't he? So what if he needed lots of rest and swallowed a pharmacy-load of pills every day just to keep him going? Muffin didn't care a hoot about any of that. It was irrelevant. She had found her family and couldn't be happier. Despite the chaos of her arrival, and the distinct disharmony of her settling-in period, Muffin immediately lifted the mood of the entire household. Like Molly, she represented freshness, joy and wonder at a new and unfolding world.

A friend of ours confided, years later, that it used to make him squirm, the way Molly would launch herself at Tim for a cuddle, bombarding him with toys and insisting that he play with her, regardless of stitches, drips, oxygen canisters or feeding tubes. 'She was remorseless,' he said, 'but Tim didn't seem to mind a bit.'

The same was true with the dog: like Molly, she carried on regardless. Tim might be fragile, but that didn't mean that those around him couldn't blossom and thrive. After all, he could still get in a fair few walks and Tuggy Toy games first, could he not? In a human world of mental confusion, the constant prescience of death and an awareness of possible disaster round every corner, this is the great gift of animals: their sublime lack of awareness and worry; their innate enthusiasm to play and run and eat and drink regardless; their undiluted ability to live. Watching Muffin as a young, beautiful and irrepressible dog reminded us all as a family – most particularly, Tim, in his darkest hour – how to live too.

Chapter Three

Sickness and Health

My dog comes to resemble Leonard Cohen more and more. Cohen is beautifully rueful about getting old. In 'The Tower of Song', he tells it straight. His hair is faded. His friends have disappeared. The pleasure zones of his body are rusting away. Lately, a few of the old dogs in the wood have been noticeably absent. Getting to the wood is a major triumph anyway. The arthritis keeps us away. We know just what you mean, Leonard.

By some miracle Muffin has made it through another winter, but at a cost. It is now 2012. With the new year has come more debilitation. She is disorientated, almost completely deaf, nearly blind, and now has arthritis in her lower spine, as well as her hips, making her unsteady on her legs and occasionally incontinent. Still, the vet seems pleased with her. I cannot quite work out why. Frankly, my dog can be unsettling to be around these days. Frequently she looks at me with incomprehension in her eyes. 'How did it get to this?' 'Who am I, and what am I doing here?' 'And who the hell are *you*?' But she still scoffs her dinner, still stretches out luxuriously for long, dreamless sleeps, a half smile playing on her black lips – a smile that tells me it is not yet time to call it a day. Most of her coat remains jet black, but there is plenty of grey around her muzzle, and long, silver-white hairs peeking through the length of her black shiny back.

Norman MacCaig has written a fine poem, 'Praise of a Collie', with single lines and a life history that speak perfectly of Muffin. Welsh sheepdog Lassie, writes the poet, had been unconscionably swift of paw, outlasting her offspring with a fierce vitality. She seemed immortal in her valour and youthfulness. 'She flowed through fences like a piece of black wind.' But the end, when it came, was brutal. She got old and lame, and the farmer, though he loved her, had to shoot her dead.

There will be no gun for Muffin, but I see a similar startling gear change from young to old. Until Muffin was twelve, she seemed utterly untouchable in her bounce and swing. Since then, it is a strange new ailment – cough, stagger, lurch – with every day that passes.

It is dogs who remind us of our own mortality. This is the poignancy of our connection, human to canine. In ten years or so, we watch them grow – and we see them grow old – with such undue speed. John Grogan writes with sweet candour of just such a scenario, in his story of one wayward Labrador retriever, *Marley and Me*. He recalls the first time that Marley failed to make it on their usual steep morning climb, and had to take a breather halfway up the slope. As he looked down at his dog, he noticed, 'His whole muzzle and a good part of his brow had turned from buff to white. Without us quite realizing it, our eternal puppy had become a senior citizen . . . Age sneaks up on us all, but it sneaks up on a dog with a swiftness that is both breathtaking and sobering.'

When I first got Muffin, I noticed a friend's mother walking lonely up the hill. She told me she had just had their beloved Alsatian put down and was stricken with sadness. She looked down at Muffin, young, eager, healthy and fit, and said, 'She will break your heart.' I never forgot those words. They have haunted me, with their simple desolation, down the years. And now, here we are, in the blink of an eye, on the brink of that precipice ourselves.

Once upon a time, Muffin did a marvellous thing. It is hard to imagine, looking at her now, soft and crumpled little old lady that she is. But in her prime, she helped a sick and depressed man become well again – in his mind, if not his body. As a very new dog, Muffin relied on me to be some kind of surrogate mother, but after the first few weeks, it was clear to her where her true allegiance lay. She soon became Tim's chief ally and companion. Despite the rocky start to their friendship – Tim's fastidious nature in complete opposition to her animal profligacy – it did not take them long to form a bond that lasted for the next four years, the last four years of Tim's life. She was there on our last visit to him at the hospice, there to share our incomprehension that he was never coming back. There, too, to help us recover from his loss – but that is another chapter in her ordinary but remarkable life. I will be forever grateful to her for the pleasure she gave to Tim, at a time when his withdrawal from the regular channels of human interaction was extreme and intransigent.

Biologist John Bradshaw once again illuminates, in his book *In Defence of Dogs*.

'Cooperation,' writes Bradshaw, 'in dogs as well as in humans, tends to favour transparency. For their ancestor, the wolf, sustaining the family unit is essential to survival, so it benefits everyone to know how everyone else is feeling ... hence both *Homo sapiens* and *Canis lupus* alike usually show their emotions openly, although wolves (and dogs) use their whole bodies, not just their faces, to communicate their emotional state.' In other words, we understand each other, human and dog. There is a pay-off for both species: we help each other to thrive. Muffin certainly did that for Tim. She loved him, and he her.

Sandy – she of the fabulous, feathery tail – did a long stint as a PAT (Pets As Therapy) dog. She and her owner Maggie visited people in residential care. One very isolated man would see Sandy, even when he refused all human visitors, and the presence of the dog triggered memories and sensory perceptions in sufferers of Alzheimer's, stroke patients and the severely physically impaired.

'One posh old lady,' says Maggie, 'hated being in the care home. We would have the same conversation every time – how Sandy reminded her of a spaniel she had as a child, whose ears would collect clumps of ice when they went for walks in the winter snow. And there was a woman in her thirties who was so badly paralysed she could hardly swallow. I used to take her hand and place it on the dog's back.'

In the end, Sandy retired early from her PAT duties. She began to find the endless attention – the bottomless well of need – too stressful. But, at eighteen, she still fulfils a powerful therapeutic function for Maggie herself. 'I look at her sometimes and it's a soul-to-soul moment. I see the love in her eyes. The fact that I'm a human and she's a dog is immaterial. When my dad died and when I've been ill myself, it's extremely comforting to have her there. I think of her as my friend.'

Muffin and Tim became best buddies during the first year that she was with us, a process speeded up by Tim's decision to stop the arduous daily commute to Bradford, where his office was, and begin working from home. Although terminally ill, his health was reasonably stable throughout 2000. He could eat well and was fit enough to walk. Thus began the epic exercise routine for man and dog, focused around long rambling excursions to the local wood and park. Leeds is blessed with an abundance of green. North-east Leeds, where we live, is particularly leafy. Walk a mile or so in any direction (except south to the inner city) and you find yourself on grass, by water, under trees. Muffin and Tim took full advantage of it all. Getting a dog had been a boyhood dream. It took him forty-three years to achieve it, but he got there in the end. What an odd couple they made: one diminutive black and tan floppy-eared mongrel, set against a big, broad, blond fellow of six foot five – little and large. His feet were almost as large as her entire body! But they were, in every other regard, a perfect match.

As mother and chief keeper-of-the-household, I was in a state of permanent busyness back then. Disaster had struck, in the form of the cancer, and I was always on the alert for new catastrophes. This was not a perfect precondition for playfulness. For Tim, it was different. Ever on duty, in my caretaker's role, I was afraid of distraction; Tim, in his depleted, invaded state, yearned for it. Muffin became his perfect foil. A ritual began of the twice-daily walk. For other dog owners, this might be a chore. For Tim, it was a saving grace. He walked to escape – the house, his cancer, all his domestic and work obligations, himself. Muffin walked for pure pleasure. She had phenomenal, boundless energy as a youngster, and could run – tirelessly – for miles and miles.

Slowly, the dog's enthusiasm infected the man. He bought proper walking boots. He kitted himself out with thick jackets, waterproof trousers. No matter what the weather – and it can be unbelievably foul up here on our high northern hills – the walk was an immovable fixture in his calendar. He set off each day with determination and vigour, the little dog bouncing happily by his side. Sometimes I went with them, but I could tell that it was not the same. The man and the dog developed a telepathic communication, finely tuned, one to the other, and a third person . . . well, frankly, I slowed them down, put a spoke in their smooth-running wheel. I took the hint and stayed away.

A major part of the walk was one particular, inexhaustible game: fetch. Muffin had a passion for sticks and would go rooting for the biggest, knottiest specimen she could find, as soon as she set foot in the wood. From then on, it was relentless. She would bring the stick to Tim and demand that he throw it for her. Muffin compensated in height for what she could not achieve in distance: she had an ability to propel herself from concrete, and a standing start, directly up into the air, like a rocket from its launcher. Tim had a massively powerful thrust in his upper arm, cancer or not, and got the same obsessive-compulsive delight as his dog from the endless repetition of throw and fetch, throw and fetch, throw and fetch. And so they proceeded through the wood, with only the occasional diversion – when Muffin careered off to chase a squirrel or investigate a deeply hidden aroma beneath the bracken and the brambles – putting them off their peculiarly single-minded and deeply monotonous sport.

Neither participant knew how to stop. Muffin would be exhausted, panting, tongue lolling, blood and drool streaked across her chops, and still she would be dragging some old stick back from the undergrowth and demanding it be thrown again. The pair of them used to come home looking as if they had been on an all-night bender, mud and damp woody bits streaked across their bodies, the smell of fresh air penetrating deep into fur, skin, vessels and nerves. Tim could hardly speak sometimes, he was so tired. But happy – very happy.

If they both wanted to inject extra mileage into the walk, the stick would be replaced by a tennis ball. Muffin never quite got the hang of the bounce. She saw the ball hit the ground, but the dynamics of its rise into the air thereafter was quite beyond her. She would stand, stock still, bewildered. Then a distant thud alerted her to the fact that the ball had descended again, and had landed in the biggest pile of brambles, tree stumps, moss, fungi and dead grass imaginable. She invariably found it, nonetheless, and came back, triumphant, wearing half the wood's greenery in her feathery ears and tail.

Despite my brief moment of sporting glory in the primary school rounders team, I have, my entire life, failed to see the significance of ball games. God knows I have been exposed to them enough. I come from a family of noisy males, the honourable exception being my mother, though she was the noisiest of the lot. My childhood was dominated by cricket in the summer, football all winter; there was no escape. On a hot summer's day, the curtains were firmly drawn in the front room and the television was on full blast – some pesky international fixture or other – with my brothers and occasional friends sprawled in lethargic assortment across sofas and on floors. Out in the garden, there was my father on the sunlounger, in residence under the tamarisk tree, radio turned up full volume and indelibly tuned to *Test Match Special*. For a particular treat, we would drive to Cressing Cricket Club and watch a live exposition of leather on willow. The thwack of the ball, the groans of disbelief and sporadic distant applause as some poor batsman got run out punctuate all my early memories, as does my mother's valiant refusal to succumb to the tyranny of the cricket teas, the cricket widow's rota of boredom and despair.

It is, then, a supreme irony that I married a man whose addiction to sport was, if anything, even more extreme. My middle brother and my dad were active participants down the years, but Tim always preferred a ringside seat. He was a consummate spectator. So the ball games in the wood – and in our little garden, outside the back door – were a tremendous release of pent-up energy accumulated down forty-odd years.

These games seem like a male obsession. I saw the same pattern three times: first, with Tim, on our leafy local walks; second, with my brother (another frustrated dog lover), when we took the young dog south to visit him; and third, with my nephew in Newcastle, who used to run Muffin so hard, armed with a battery of balls, frisbees and rope toys, that I feared for her safety. Her paws were like worn-out threads when we came back from seeing him. He was remorseless. Now he has a young dog of his own that he tortures with equal enthusiasm – and mutual satisfaction.

Inside the house, the growing bond between man and new dog proceeded at a quieter pace. Tim, even during his well phases, was both a television addict and a chronic insomniac. I shared neither affliction, but Muffin was happy to participate in both. She would watch all the late-night news, the edgy dramas, the avant-garde films and documentaries, with an avidity quite equal to that of her master. She was very well versed in current affairs. Although her capacity for snoozing, in true canine fashion, has always been enthusiastic and prodigious, she is adaptable too. When Tim came trotting downstairs at 2 a.m., some demon or other at his heels, and sleep having eluded him yet again, Muffin would rouse herself from her bed and be his willing, mute companion. Midnight snacks were consumed. Tea was brewed. Whiskey snifters gulped down greedily. Hour after silent hour went by. The isolation of the man was softly mitigated by his constant canine companion. The great glory of a dog is this: she is always ready to go with the flow. The needs of her master may be difficult and ever changing, but her own needs are simple – to accompany and to please.

The surface of things, in a dog's life, is just a fraction of the full story – the tip of a very tall mountain. When I look at dogs and their owners, it seems such a straightforward thing: humans and their animal pets, trotting side by side through their lives. The real beauty of the dog is in what lies beneath. There is an invisible connecting cord, a kind of hard-wired intuition, which emanates from a dog towards its master. This canine radar goes far deeper than words can ever express. I used to drive my poor husband wild with inquiry. How was he? What was he thinking? What could I do to make things better? Muffin short-circuited all of that. She asked nothing, made no demands. Her only function was to *be alongside*, whatever the terrain. There is a world of sophistication in this kind of simplicity. We just cannot reach it from within our human limitations.

In Philip Pullman's philosophical fantasy trilogy *His Dark Materials*, he touches on the significance of animals for the health of the human psyche. His great invention is the 'daemon', or animal spirit, which assumes corporeal form and accompanies each human on their life's journey, as a kind of manifestation of their soul. Splitting someone from their daemon results in great psychic pain, a sort of living death. Many of the characters, as befits their extravagant natures, have beautiful and exotic daemons: heroine Lyra has a pine marten; her cruel and powerful mother has a golden monkey; her emperor father, a snow leopard. Lyra's best friend, Roger, who is both heroic and doomed in his loyalty towards her, is not an exceptional character; he is ordinary and loving. His daemon? A little terrier called Salcilia. Give me that little dog over the cold-eyed, scheming monkey any day.

The first year of Muffin's life with us passed in a sort of happy haze of newness and vitality. I saw a visible change in Tim's demeanour, and Muffin grew from a sad, neglected little individual to a bonny, happy, healthy young dog. There would be another golden time, in 2002, when Tim had an unexpected resurgence in strength and well-being, but as the year 2000 came to a close, things were changing for the worst.

Tim had been free of treatment for a couple of years, and the significant tumours pressing down on his left lung and encroaching on his heart were quiescent. He learned to operate with one lung (the other one had been substantially removed in

1994, in the initial surgery to debulk the original tumour), and he coped with a mass of scar tissue causing pain and discomfort, both internally and externally. He also learned how to recover from industrial amounts of chemotherapy and a battering of radiotherapy, all in the name of cheating the encroaching cancer. But something was happening inside: his body was beginning to cave under the many assaults made on it through the past seven years.

As 2001 progressed, his appetite dwindled to nothing. He developed a chronic and unproductive cough. He lost weight. Always handsome and substantial, he became thin and gaunt. He hardly slept. He looked haunted by his past – and by the future. He developed a nervous aversion to company, became reclusive and shy. He never wanted to go out, and would see only his family, or very close friends, and even then rarely, reluctantly. The world was closing in on him. Worst of all, his capacity for exercise disappeared. He stopped walking the dog – that became my duty. He would hardly even sit outside. The house became his fortress. More acute than any of the physical symptoms was the blanket of depression that fell over him at this time. It was this persistent darkness of mood that was the hardest for those around him to deal with. Of the three of us, I handled it the worst. Molly was stalwart, and got through to him more than anyone else, but the one who bore it with least complaint, and most success, was Muffin.

Dogs know about sadness. Perhaps dogs who have been sad in their early lives, like Muffin, know about it better than any.

There is an insightful passage in Tolstoy's *Anna Karenina* that most touchingly demonstrates this knowledge. Konstantin Levin has returned to his country estate after being rejected in marriage by Kitty, the love of his life. His dog Laska immediately senses that something is wrong.

> Old Laska ... approached him and, putting her head under his hand, whined plaintively, asking to be patted.
>
> 'She all but speaks,' said Agatha Mikhaylovna [the housekeeper]. 'She is only a dog, but she understands that her master has come back feeling depressed ...'
>
> Laska kept pushing her head under his hand. He patted her a little, and she curled up at his feet with her head on her outstretched hind paw. And to show that all was now well and satisfactory, she slightly opened her mouth, smacked her sticky lips, and, drawing them more closely over her old teeth, lay still in blissful peace.

In just such a manner of sweet and graceful acceptance, Muffin adjusted her step to Tim's, as he entered this new and dark phase of his illness. It was a greater shock for her than for the rest of us. She didn't have the benefit of spoken diagnoses and doctors' consultations. All she could do was read the information written on her master's face, see the falter in his once enormous stride, and sense the atmosphere gathering like storm clouds inside the family home. The news, as she smelt and felt it, was bad. Gone were the two-hour hikes, and the hilarious tug-of-war contests, in which she held on so tightly to her toy – her jaw in a vice-like grip – that Tim would lift her clear of the ground, all four paws dangling in mid-air glory. Finished was the hide-and-seek hilarity of the Brown Bag Game, a ritual learned from dog-lover friends in Ireland, in which a Bonio or chocolate dog treat was hidden in a paper bag somewhere about the house, sending Muffin into a frenzy of hunting, until the treasure was found, the bag ripped apart by tooth and claw, and the prize consumed with a theatrical relish. But it is not in a dog's nature to complain. Muffin simply took her cue from the clues around her, and stepped into her most important job yet: nurse's assistant and convalescent's companion. It is the role she seems to have been born for, because she managed it so well.

In my house growing up, first came two cats and then the dog – and later a tribe of white mice and a jar full of stick insects, but that's another story. If you wanted action and adventure, you called the dog, who would leap on your head with excitement. If you needed peace and quiet, one of the cats was your pal. The detached serenity of the feline is perfectly suited to the hushed atmosphere of a sickroom, their refusal to concern themselves with human mood and expectation making them calm companions even in the most catastrophic of cases. Consummately selfish, they are also wonderfully soothing. As Theresa Mancuso puts it, in *Cats Do It Better Than People*: 'The sound of the cat mesmerises, calms the chattering mind, stills the anxious heart.'

On the face of it, Muffin, by comparison, was the worst candidate for carer imaginable: she was nervous, hyperactive, wired for sound. She jumped out of her skin when anyone knocked at the door. Delivery-men, refuse lorries and thunder-storms left her both furious and quaking – an uncomfortable combination. She hated being alone. She was not self-contained in the slightest degree – any cat she met during the course of her honourable career regarded her with utter contempt. But out of this wrecked little bundle came a creature of great equanimity and consolation.

She learned to take her cue entirely from Tim. If it were a good day, she would totter down the road with him, just to get a little fresh air and feel the breeze blowing on their faces. If it were warm outside, she would sit by his deckchair and keep a kind of guard, as he read the paper, listened to the radio, dozed and dreamed. If things were bad and the pain or sickness descended, Muffin simply shifted her position to the bottom of the sofa or the end of the bed. On these occasions, quietness and fortitude would fall upon the dog. She lay for hours at a time simply bearing witness. Occasionally she would stir, moving closer to lick his hand gently or to let him stroke her head, her silky ears. Her eyes, when they were open, were like dark pools, absorbing the atmosphere and drawing the suffering away from him and into herself – or so it seemed.

There are cases of dogs developing cancers themselves when they have been around cancer sufferers for long enough. Remembering Muffin's absorption in Tim's illness, I can well believe it. A dog will do *anything* for the owner it loves. The lines of separation – at a physical and a psychic level – sometimes become very blurred. The year 2001 was one of those times for Muffin.

Tim always maintained that he knew when the cancer was active again after a period of remission. 'I get a metallic taste in my mouth,' he said, 'and a weird smell and sensation in my nose, like burning rubber.' Muffin was also sensitive to the progress of his disease. As biologist John Bradshaw writes, 'Dogs live in a world that is dominated by their sense of smell – a world that is quite unlike ours, which is constructed around what we see.' This extraordinary sense of smell in canines has been used to detect melanomas, ovarian and bladder tumours. Dogs' ability to detect subtle changes in body odour has led to them being trained to sound the alert for impending diabetic and epileptic seizures. It is possible that Muffin could both feel and smell Tim's cancer. That is quite a burden for one little dog to carry.

I claim no special powers for Muffin. She is a supremely ordinary dog, with more than her fair share of disgusting habits – a fixation with rubbish bins and excrement coming close to the top of the list. Just this week, I came home to find the contents of the kitchen bin strewn across the floor, and followed the trail of destruction into the hall, where I found the dog lying in her basket, with the swing lid of the bin jammed over her head, front paws and chest! She looked quite cosy, wearing it like the top half of a plastic bikini. On the evidence of this alone, her admission into the saintly section of dog heaven seems doubtful. She is not even particularly bright, with another million or so brain cells biting the dust when she bangs her head on the same table leg for the third time in one afternoon. I merely draw attention to the kind of skills that have been shown by generations of dogs through the ages, and used in the service of the owners they love. None of this is new.

In 800 BCE, Homer created his labyrinthine tale *The Odyssey*, the story of Odysseus's long journey home to Ithaca after the end of the ten-year Trojan War. Everyone assumes that he has died. Even his wife Penelope and son Telemachus, who are busy fighting off suitors to be his successor, have given up on him. When Odysseus does finally make it back, he is in deep disguise as a beggar, to avoid attack. Not a single person recognises him. But an old dog, lying sick and neglected on a pile of cow dung by the city gates, lifts up his gaze in instant recognition. Odysseus knows in his heart who this dog is. 'This was Argos, whom Odysseus had bred before setting out for Troy ... As soon as he saw Odysseus standing there, he dropped his ears and wagged his tail, but he could not get close up to his master ... When Odysseus saw the dog on the other side of the yard, he dashed a tear from his eyes ... and said: "What a noble hound that is ...'"

Master and dog know each other in a heartbeat, deeply changed and disfigured by age and experience though they both are. Just as people on their deathbed seem to choose the moment of death, waiting for the last meeting with someone special, or for some unfinished business to be completed before they die, the

faithful Argos, age-tattered and lice-infested as he was, obviously had a mission of his own. Ignored and reviled by everyone
around him, he nonetheless kept guard by the stable door, waiting only for the master's return. As soon as he saw Odysseus
pass safely back through the gates of his estate, the old dog died.
His long watch was over.

It is a long-standing practice to give a pet to someone who is
sick or sad in an effort to raise their spirits. Dogs have proved
themselves particularly well suited to the task. An actor friend
bought a little dog for his mother after the death of his father.
She resisted the notion vehemently at first – 'Such a tie ... I
won't be able to look after it properly ...' – but he insisted.
Eventually she gave in. The dog arrived, and it was love at first
sight. Soon the pair of them were roaming the hills of their
neighbourhood, making friends, both canine and human,
whereas before she had been housebound, isolated and bereft.

Illustrious examples of such companionship abound in con-
temporary literature, as well as in the classics. Virginia Woolf
wrote a whole book based on the life of a real spaniel called
Flush, the beloved pet of the poet Elizabeth Barrett Browning,
given to her after she suffered prolonged, traumatic grief at the
drowning of her favourite brother, Edward. The bereavement
sent Elizabeth into a virtually catatonic state. She retired to her
sofa and languished under blankets and behind closed curtains,
in a self-elected retreat from the world.

'Spaniels are by nature sympathetic,' writes Woolf, and that
does seem to be the case. All the spaniels I have known,

including Muffin, weave around their owners' ankles in a never-ending quest to get as close as they possibly can to the object of their affection. This fits them especially for the sickroom. Flush was a mere puppy when he went to live with Elizabeth, and he relished the daily outings with her maid, along the seafront in Torquay, as any self-respecting hound would. But he adapted immediately to different demands. 'Once back with his mistress . . . he lay so motionless that the loudest sound in the room was his breathing.' Woolf is clear about the sacrifice Flush made: all his natural instincts to run and play were thwarted in his adopted role as Elizabeth's companion, a bereavement therapist in canine form. But she is also clear that his sacrifice was a willing one. He knew what was expected of him, and he rose to the occasion magnificently.

The novel, like its hero called *Flush*, was published in 1933, and is an unusual attempt to enter the mind of an animal and see the world from the canine point of view. It is one of the few pieces of fiction I have read that succeeds, without undue whimsy or sentimentality, in evoking the inner world of a dog with sympathetic conviction.

So much about Flush reminds me of my own dog. Both animals rendered selfless service to the owners who depended on them; each one adapted their behaviour according to the changing circumstances around them, without falter or complaint. In Flush's case, he had to get used, first, to confinement in a darkened sickroom, then to the arrival of Robert Browning, Elizabeth's eventual lover – provoking much jealousy and consternation. (Both of these emotions are highly articulated in every dog I have known.) Then Flush copes with a long sea journey to Italy, where he, like his mistress, enjoys a rich and rewarding new life. Italy is full of colour and delight. Flush leads a much freer life here, and Elizabeth is far less dependent on him, now that she has her beloved Robert by her side. And so he enters, in Woolf's imagination, the most carefree and joyful years of his life. Muffin, in her turn, learned to be quiet and still, padding softly through the bedroom of a sick and dying man. The energy stored during those long hours and days was later released, after Tim's death, in a new round of walks and play-time. The most difficult part of her working life was now over, with a long, happy retirement still to come. Woolf understands the quintessential quality of dog. She describes it with luscious precision: 'Where Mrs Browning saw, [Flush] smelt, where she wrote, he snuffed ... Love was chiefly smell ... [And] not a single one of his myriad sensations ever submitted itself to the deformity of words.'

Tim was a man of few words. The connection he made with Muffin was perfect for him, particularly at the time of his life when she came bounding in. Overcome by sickness, pain and the preparation for death, a death he knew was coming ten years ahead of its arrival, what could be more consoling than a mute, furry animal at his side, demanding nothing, except to be there. Human beings want to tug at the dying man's sleeve, 'Don't go!' implicit in every gesture; dogs cut right through such messy adhesion.

A friend of mine, who had been through a long and difficult illness, and was now convalescing – and suffering consequent mood swings and bouts of debilitating lethargy – went for a lesson in the Alexander technique to realign her back and neck. Lying semi-supine on the teacher's table, she was startled to tears when the teacher suddenly said, 'You know, you need to find yourself a dog. They're good companions. None of that yabber yabber yabber you get with people.'

Tim was never a fan of the yabber yabber yabber. By the end of 2001, he and Muffin had spent hundreds of silent hours, just lying or sitting still, while I whirled around like a dervish, keeping our family together. Summer had been the worst time. It was fiendishly hot. Tim's appetite had completely disappeared. The outline of his skeleton began to be etched clearly beneath his skin. The most he could manage in a day was to move outside, like a whisper, and take up residence in a reclining chair, under the shade of the little apple tree. There he would slump for hours on end, sometimes reading, sometimes lost in a kind of reverie or trance. Muffin, of course, was with him under that tree.

She was faithful, no question, but she was not averse to manipulating the situation to her advantage. Tim never put her on the lead, expecting her to stay with him without command. This she did, quite happily. But Tim had a habit of dozing off, particularly mid-afternoon. This is when I went to collect Molly from primary school. Sometimes the dog came too, but on one particular occasion, she stayed at home with Tim in the front garden.

'Look out for the dog,' I called before I left.

Tim, his nose buried deep in his newspaper, Muffin regarding me insouciantly from under his feet, barely looked up, as he called back carelessly, 'OK!'

Half an hour later, when I got back, Tim was in exactly the same position, but where Muffin had lain there was a patch of flattened grass and a distinct absence of dog. 'Where's Muffin?' I asked, a little panicked – not since her very early days had she run away.

'She's here, isn't she?' he replied lazily, peering over the top of his ubiquitous paper. Well, no, she wasn't.

At that precise moment, as if timed by the clock, just as I was beginning to scream her name, Muffin came flying along the street from the direction of Fairy Woods, ears streaming, tail waving, pushing herself through the little gap between gate and tree and skidding to a halt at my feet. Goodness knows how long she had been hanging out with the wild things in the wood, or what she had been up to. All I can say is: who can blame her? Dogs may be built for dedication and service, but they are also wired for fun. My dog has enjoyed her share of both.

Modern medicine is a marvellous thing. When Tim had undergone radiotherapy in 1997, he also took large quantities of steroids as a complementary treatment. The side-effects of such high doses can be extreme, and Tim got the lot: his weight ballooned, his face took on the moon shape sometimes associated with steroid use and – most scary of all – he began to hallucinate and suffer psychotic episodes. Determined to come off the drugs, he went through a long and difficult process, cutting down his dosage by minute amounts to avoid withdrawal symptoms, until at last he was free. This experience made him understandably wary of the very word 'steroid'. So, when he first started to waste away in 2001, he was reluctant to take anything that might lead to a similar addictive reaction. But as things got worse and he became a spectre of his former self, the cancer attacking him from the inside out, he agreed to take a low dose of steroids again as an aid to appetite and an anti-inflammatory. The result was remarkable: his mood lifted, his appetite returned, he gained weight – but only a reasonable amount. His face returned to its normal handsome proportions. In short, under the same medical regime as before, but with a drastically reduced dosage, he blossomed and thrived. If the year 2001 had been a nightmare year, then 2002 was like the return of spring after a long, hard winter.

Everyone in the house was happy again. I had my husband back, Molly had her dad and Muffin her playmate. The games began in earnest and proper walks were resumed. If anything, Muffin and Tim stayed out longer than ever. Being such a night bird, he particularly liked walking after dark. This did not thrill me. Our estate had its share of nasty boys at that time, and Gipton Wood, his usual stamping-ground, is a natural haunt for high jinks, with plenty of green cover and dark, dark corners. I asked him not to be out so long, but he shrugged me off. For a man with a death sentence, I suppose nothing seems threatening any more. I used to console myself that the dog would protect him, though Tim wasn't sure. 'I'm under no illusions about her self-defence qualities,' he said, looking down at the diminutive form of his dog. I thought differently. Muffin had sharp teeth and a territorial instinct – and Tim was *prime* territory to her. I think she would have done serious damage to anyone who attacked her master: one bright leap and she could reach a man's genitals and snap them off with ease.

We travelled a lot – by our somewhat ankle-shackled standards – in 2002: Ireland, Cornwall, London, city streets, seaside and moorland. Sometimes the dog was with us, sometimes not. (She even did her share of travel on the London Underground, but, like the rest of humanity, she was not a fan.) This was the year she developed a love affair with a different family: the start of a series of three 'foster homes', where, down the years, Muffin would make herself comfortable with her characteristic mix of charm and cheekiness. Tim's cousins, Roger and Rose, were massive dog fans. Their appetite for walks and play was equal to ours and beyond. They soon fell in love with Muffin and she with them.

Each time we picked her up at the end of a week away, she seemed to have acquired a new toy, a new bag of treats, a new trick. Her favourite was 'Give me the paw'. She would trot into the kitchen, with a keen, expectant air, quite in the mood for a beef-flavoured Schmackos bar and only too aware how to get one. Down she would sit, head erect, paws neat and tidy, ears all fluffed and silky. 'Give me the paw!' I would say (as instructed by Rose), and up would shoot her right paw, where it hovered in the air, elegantly crooked, ready to shake hands. Trick completed, she would carry her treat triumphantly to her basket in the hall and wolf it down in one. Happy owner, smug dog. These humans are so easy.

She always looked particularly sleek and healthy after staying in her Newcastle lodgings. Rose would groom her every day – putting me quite to shame. And despite all our strict injunctions on the plainness of her diet, I am certain a fair amount of prime beef and bacon found its way into Muffin's ever-open mouth. 'Whoops, my hand must have slipped while I was carving.' Pull the other one, Rose. Everyone wants people to love their child the way they do, though they know in their hearts what a tall order that is; it is the same with animals. Rose and Roger really *did* love Muffin, finding qualities in her we didn't know existed, and singing her praises to an embarrassing degree. It was a pleasure to leave her in such safe hands. The reward on our return was a dog simply exploding with joy and well-being.

The honeymoon couldn't last for long. In 2003 Tim was failing again. This time, there would be no miraculous turnaround. In his final year, Muffin, like the rest of the family, learned to share her master with a succession of nurses and healthcare professionals, which, frankly, she was rather reluctant to do. She was used to being ward sister, and she had no confidence in all these new characters slapping tubes on his chest and needles in his arms. The hospital had ceded care to the local hospice. We were visited regularly by Macmillan nurses, and Tim became first an outpatient and then a resident on one of the wards.

Hospices are remarkable places. Not only are the patients cosseted in first-class accommodation, more like a hotel than a clinic for the terminally ill, but the entire family are looked after too. In our case, the family included a dog. We expected that she would have to stay at home, but that wasn't the case. Dogs were welcome – indeed, highly prized – visitors on the wards and in the day-care unit. We were positively encouraged to bring her along.

My daughter Molly, after a lifetime of tents and bed and breakfast dives, has a passion for posh hotels. There is fascination in rarity! The hospice, with its free machines dispensing coffee and hot chocolate, its lounges with deep, comfy chairs and glossy magazines, was a kind of paradise to her. The nightmare of her father's decline was cushioned by the elegant surroundings, the calm and cheerful staff, and the obvious ease and relief that Tim felt at being there. We all felt safe, at a perilous time in our lives, and I shall never stop being grateful for that. Best of all, the dog came too.

Tim was admitted in September, and stayed until his death on 8 January. Within a few days of his being there, Muffin was a recognised and much-fussed fixture. The nurses were crazy about her. Other visitors were visibly cheered by her presence. The patients, most of all, appreciated her visits. This sounds back to front, but in any kind of institution for work, business or health, a child – or a dog – is a civilising force. I felt this more than ever at the hospice. It was such a contrast to the sterile wards of the general hospitals we had come to loathe. Muffin, of course, took it all for granted. So long as she got to see Tim, everything was just fine by her.

There are two critical times in a person's life: when they enter it and when they leave. Tim and I experienced one birth – Molly's – and one death – Tim's – together. There is no greater privilege than watching the gates of change swing open. Molly's birth was long and arduous. After nearly two days in labour, she started to be born, but turned her head into the breech position at the last minute, causing panic and high-speed reaction among the medical staff, and a consequent panoply of high-tech interventions. When she actually arrived, I was utterly exhausted and delirious with joy. Tim had fallen asleep several times during the long labour – to my disgust. He, too, was absolutely spent. But how he loved that little baby. I have a photograph of him holding her, the day we brought her home. He is gazing at her in perplexed wonder, arms crooked in an awkward and exaggerated protectiveness. There is mystery and revelation mixed, in the astonished expression on his face.

Shortly before he had his cancer diagnosis, eighteen months later, he had a curious dream. He was climbing a high and difficult mountain with an old college friend. Suddenly there was a landslide: one of the rocks that came roaring down struck him on the left shoulder with considerable force (this was the site of the tumour soon to be diagnosed – under his left shoulder). The scene then switched to a hospital, where a doctor was peering at a Petri dish. Slowly, deep in the dish, faces began to appear – the faces of babies – and the clearest, brightest face of all was Molly's. When Tim described this dream to me, he spoke of the profound joy the face of Molly produced in him as he dreamed. There was a warning of danger here – the blow to the shoulder, the life-threatening landslide – and, in the next instant, a reminder of hope and new beginnings. Tim never spoke of his dreams again, but this one kept him company for the rest of his life.

Although I was just a spectator at Tim's dying, the experience felt as profoundly physical, as gut-wrenching and turbulent, as Molly's birth. After a peaceful few weeks in his hospice room – a time when he felt so free of personal and domestic obligation that he enjoyed some rich and solitary moments, reading, listening to his favourite music and watching films – the day came when the cancer would claim him for good. After a Christmas shared between hospice and home, with brief visits to us and to his parents, a process made arduous by oxygen cylinders, drips and wheelchairs, January 2004 brought the final reckoning. Tim's breathing was getting more and more laboured. He coughed in painful convulsions and needed increasing amounts of oxygen, as well as morphine for the pain.

Everything was a blur. We were all in a kind of suspended animation, as Tim made his final transition from life to death. In the few pictures I have of this time, everyone looks white and strained beyond endurance, and at the edges of a couple of images, there she is, a contrasting black, furry figure amongst all the anxious humans – Muffin. She was entirely undemanding at this time. She went unwalked and mostly ignored in an atmosphere of permanent crisis. Even in these extremes, she played her part.

When it was clear that Tim wouldn't last out for much longer, Molly went to stay with her aunt for a little relief and relaxation. Muffin, meanwhile, came with me to the hospice more and more frequently. In the last week of Tim's life, we stayed the night a couple of times, me on a fold-out bed by the window, Muffin in her basket between Tim's bed and mine, alert, as ever, in her duties towards us both.

With us, she was calm and sweet. To the nurses, she was respectful. But when the doctors arrived, she was like a little Rottweiler, growling and barking at the liberties they took with her master. What on earth did she suspect them of doing? Their aim was to ease his suffering, and if their medication made dying gentler, too, then no one was about to complain – Tim had gone through enough; no one, that is, except Muffin. It got embarrassing. I found myself clamping her complaining muzzle shut the minute the beleaguered medics put their heads tentatively round the door. 'Sorry, she isn't normally like this. She's quite a nice dog, really.'

It is a common occurrence for humans to become angry when a loved one dies. The protest and denial is loud. Why could the hospital not have acted quicker? If only the GP had referred them sooner. Why were the drugs so slow acting, and why did the surgery come so late? The list of 'maybes' is endless, but the truth is simple: death cannot be cheated or deferred. It comes in its own time. Muffin could howl at the moon as much as she wanted, but Tim's time was upon him.

Animals often retreat to die alone. The process of separation – of life from death, of the physical from the psychic body, of matter into energy or spirit – can occur so much more smoothly if it happens alone. The same is true with people. Once the final meetings have taken place, and unfinished business concluded, it is a sad fact that friends and relatives can be a supreme hindrance for the one who needs to die. Hospice nurses told me that it was very common for patients to choose a quiet moment, when a relative had slipped out of the room for a cup of coffee perhaps, to drift off into death, without the risk of fuss or weeping.

Molly and I had seen Tim almost every day for the length of his hospice stay. Molly came after school and they watched children's TV together. We would often eat in the hospice canteen, my appetite for cooking having almost disappeared. Afternoons and evenings revolved around the hospice bed. Yet when Tim chose to die, it was nine in the morning. The time between the phone call from the ward to say the end was imminent and his actual death was too short for me to make the brief journey from home to hospice to be with him. When I got there, he had gone. His spirit still filled the room, but his body was an empty house. I felt cheated, but not surprised. Tim was an intensely private man, and what can be more intimate than the moment of your own death?

Molly, Muffin and I had been the last to visit him the night before. Molly had bought him a gigantic muffin – double chocolate chip – and a bunch of yellow tulips. I had lifted Muffin onto the bed and placed Tim's hand on the top of her head for a last connection, man to dog. Then we left, and so did Tim.

True stories abound of dogs being faithful to their owners, even to death and well beyond. In a remarkable piece of hyperbole, George Graham Vest, an American politician and lawyer in the nineteenth century, expressed this loyalty in 'Eulogy on the Dog', which he used in his summing-up at a trial for damages, his client's foxhound, Old Drum, having been shot unjustly by a sheep farmer for being on the farmer's land. Vest's closing argument was tortuous and sentimental. Here is its apotheosis: '. . . when the last scene of all comes, and death takes the master in its embrace and his body is laid away in the cold ground . . . there by his graveside will the noble dog be found, his head between his paws, his eyes sad but open in alert watchfulness, faithful and true, even unto death.' Needless to say, Vest won his case. A statue of Old Drum stands in front of a Missouri courthouse to this day.

Most British people are familiar with the story of Greyfriars Bobby, the little Skye terrier who stood guard over his master's grave for fourteen years described earlier, but there are international dog heroes too. Consider the case of Shep, a herding dog who appeared at the Great Northern Railway Station in Fort

Benton, Montana, in 1936. No one could work out why he was there, until someone remembered that he had come first when a casket, loaded with his master's ashes, had been put aboard a train heading east. Shep kept returning to the station in wait for his master for the next six years – until he was run over by a passing train.

Railway stations have a particularly poignant role to play in these stories of death, dogs and loyalty. Hachiko, an Akita dog, who lived 1923–1935, has achieved posthumous fame for his duties towards his owner, a professor at Tokyo University. Every day, Hachiko would meet the professor at Shibuya Station after work. In May 1925, Professor Ueno did not return. He had suffered a cerebral haemorrhage and died. Poor Hachiko kept faith with his dead master for the next nine years, going to the station every day to meet the train, until his own death, when he was twelve. He became a great symbol of family loyalty in Japan. While he still lived, people fed and cared for him at the station. After his death, a statue was erected in his honour and, on 8 April every year, a ceremony of remembrance is held in his honour at Shibuya Station.

Muffin didn't have much to do with trains once we had a car, but she did her miniature version of 'meeting the train' after Tim had died. Whenever Molly and I arrived home, she would rush out to greet the car and welcome us in. Realising that we were just two, she would go back to the car and wait at the passenger door for Tim to appear. It took her some time to adjust, although not, it must be said, as long as the rest of us. Instinctively, Muffin knew – although she did not come to the funeral – that Tim was dead. With the earthy pragmatism of an animal, plus the elevated sense of duty particular to a dog, she soon turned her attention to the rest of the family. Muffin knew her job was far from over: two other people needed her support and companionship, now more than ever.

The hero of Virginia Woolf's book *Flush* has been honoured not only with his own biography, but also with a poem in his praise, this time by the owner herself, Elizabeth Barrett Browning. In the poem she pays tribute to Flush's remarkable patience at the side of her mistress's sickbed. Some of the lines could have been written for Muffin, who showed such great sympathy and respect during the years when she accompanied Tim at his most ill and incapacitated. It is hard to know if dogs grieve. They show no recognisable sign in the form of tears or audible lament, but something in the way they wait, something in the quality of their silence, gives them away. One particular lyric in Browning's poem conveys some of the strength I noticed in Muffin around the time of Tim's final illness and death:

This dog only, waited on,
Knowing that when light is gone
Love remains for shining.

Chapter Four

Death and Renewal

I t is early March 2012. The conversations I have these days are getting more difficult. Exchanges among friends – and whispered asides to the dog herself – come back, time and time again, to the question of the end. Human beings, with the curse and complication of words, can usually articulate how they are feeling. Are they in pain? Sad? Depressed? When something is expressed, a problem aired, then some hope of a solution is illuminated too. But Muffin cannot speak, and liberating and restful though this may be, it also, at times of change, creates difficulty and confusion, at least among the humans around her, who do love their words.

As a very old dog, Muffin's decline is visible, rapid and measurable, day by day, almost hour by hour. The use of her back legs is now completely unreliable. Sometimes I find her sprawled on the lino floor of the kitchen in ungainly fashion, when this clearly would not be her ideal spot for a comfy snooze. Sometimes her legs give way altogether, and she simply cannot stand. Meanwhile, her poor eyesight, when she is up on her haunches, sends her crashing into cupboards and doorposts. Encroaching deafness means that the vacuum cleaner – once a dragon of mythical proportions – holds no terrors at all; likewise she can't hear when the food bowl is rattled, a sound that once sent her into a frenzy of joyful expectation, and the deprivation of which is something Beethoven would surely have signalled with a consoling sonata. Even her sense of smell, the holy of holies, is blunted. When we stand in the garden, waiting, in wind and rain, for her to remember to pee, her nose and her gaze are now vacantly off in the middle distance, where, just a month ago, she would have been snuffling – snout deep in the grass – with an energy distilled to an almost erotic degree. There seems very little pleasure left in her daily routine. All is reduced to function, and the function itself – Eat, Sleep, Pee and Poo – is performed in the most bored and perfunctory fashion. The question I ask myself more and more is one that she cannot answer, as a human being might: Have you had enough, old friend? Is it time to call it a day?

'At least she still has a good appetite!' I said to a dog-loving friend, when asking for advice on the matter – or, rather, seeking consolation.

'Oh, that's nothing to go off!' she replied. 'They'll keep on eating regardless. It's like a reflex.'

I pressed her further. How will I know when the end has come? At what point do I finish a life that has become more about endurance than joy or satisfaction?

'I've had two dogs put to sleep,' she said, 'and each time they

'Well, I must say that the link between me and Muffin feels very faint these days,' I say. 'When I stroke her, she doesn't respond or relax like she used to. And when I tickle her muzzle, she never licks me with her tongue, where once, it was impossible to stop her ... And she hasn't wagged her tail for weeks.' I have to stop. I can feel tears forming, and anxiety growing.

What am I doing to my dog? No matter how much I tell her to let go when she is ready – as I did with each of the people I witnessed on the brink of death – maybe another message is coming through stronger. The message? DON'T GO! Please don't go.

I feel quite shaky by the end of the evening and make a decision not to talk about the dog again. People have strong views on the subject and those views are clouding my vision. I fully expect to find Muffin in a crumpled, lifeless heap when I get home, but the opposite is the case.

Three things are remarkable. One, she gets up immediately to greet me, rather than lying half-unconscious until I rouse her – and, yes, the tail is up and (feebly) waving. Two, she walks with a reasonably steady gait to the back garden and executes a swift symphony of peeing and pooing. Three, when she lies down in her bed, and I offer my hand, as always, in bedtime salutation, she opens her mouth, looks at me – and covers my palm in unexpected kisses. If dogs send clear communication right to the end of their lives, then nothing could be clearer than this. It is as if she had bugged my earlier conversation and taken swift,

let me know they had had enough.' But how? 'It w
They just made it clear that they did not want to
bodies any more.'

This was small consolation. Muffin is clearly unco
with arthritis and general old age, although the vet seem
that, while she is aching, she is not in unbearable pain. A
eyes, they tell me little of late: no beseeching, no hum
real communication. She is a blank canvas, where eloq
once poured forth like molten chocolate. I falter even m
the conversation proceeds.

'Perhaps she knows you are writing about her,' my fri
remarks. Does she feel scrutinised, obliged? Surely not. I
writing to celebrate my dog's quietly heroic, ordinary life, n
to make her stay longer than is right. Indeed, every night, wher
I say goodnight to Muffin, I whisper in her ear, 'It's OK. Your
working life is over. Stay as long as you like, because you know
that you are loved, but don't hang on for us. When you are
ready, just close your eyes, and don't wake up. That's the way
to do it. Make it easy, easy, easy on yourself.'

This conflict in me is so familiar. Here I am, loaded with the
guilt of the living, as I hover around the one who is going to die.
I felt this with my husband, then my mother and, most recently,
my father. Always the tension was there between wanting to
save, needing to hold on and desperately wanting their struggle
to be over. I feel my uncertainty over the dog pushing on me,
like a boulder over the heart, as this discussion with my friend
carries on.

aversive action. 'Not yet,' those kisses seemed to say. 'No, I'm not done yet.' And I realise that I have taken the wrong tack, as so often before. It is not me that I must trust to know how to handle the death of my dog, but, as my friend insisted, it should be left to the wisdom of the dog herself.

In his poem 'A Dog Has Died', Pablo Neruda pays touching tribute to the simple, loyal connection between him and his canine companion. There was no fuss, he writes, just friendship, all through the dog's 'sweet and shaggy life'. How apt a phrase.

Muffin is a musky, long-haired dog, with a thick black coat that moults, to torment me, all year round. With my childhood dog, Tess, autumn and spring were the coat-shedding times, but since the advent of central heating such rhythms have lost their meaning. Nonetheless, the constant nest of fur, clogging up carpet and blowing like tumbleweed across the kitchen lino, is a small price to pay for the dog's constancy and devotion.

She, it must be said, is altogether more consistent than the humans she attends. Now she is elderly and retired, Muffin has a solipsistic air: her world is small and almost entirely internal. As a younger dog, her every moment was spent guarding the space, monitoring the mood of the house, and adjusting her behaviour accordingly. During the months leading up to, and following, Tim's death, no one had much time for Muffin. But, like Neruda's dog, she never complained. She 'asked nothing', but was there, ready for duty, when duty was required. Many dogs, particularly females, are like top-of-the-range, extra-quilted kitchen towels, soaking up the tears in the atmosphere around them, then giving back something softer, easier, 'sweeter' in return.

As a child, when I was nervous or agitated, which was often, I would sit by my dog for hours and stroke her compulsively, pouring nonsense words into her ear – as if the English language itself were too potent, too painful to use – whilst Tess drank it all in with a pleasingly detached air. I think she was just happy to have the attention, whatever state I was in. Not all dogs are as acutely sensitive to sadness as Muffin seems to be. Tess was kind but careless. She barged along gaily, no matter the mayhem around her. Many other dogs I know do exactly that: bumble through their woofly lives, just waiting for the next meal, walk or playtime. Worse still are the attention-seekers: endless whining and tail wagging; rainstorms of unwanted kisses and the placing of muddy paws intrusively on laps.

Muffin is certainly no saint – she has always been noisy and fussy when people come to the door – but she is peculiarly adept at sniffing out the emotional truth, and responding to it in an appropriate and downright therapeutic way. She never lets her own personality or needs impinge when there is a crisis going on in her family.

The year 2004, when Tim died, was one long crisis, really, of catatonic shock and grief. People assume that we coped with it better because we saw it coming. There was, after all, a whole decade to prepare. But that is not the way it worked out. A train crash is still a catastrophe, even if you dreamt about it ten years earlier. Death is always, at some level, a disaster. As a result, my memories of this particular year – a year in which there were two further deaths, of my father-in-law and a beloved aunt – are dim and muted. I was exhausted, but there were things to do of an endless, bureaucratic nature (why does society force grieving people to be so practical?), and I was deeply, deeply distracted.

I know that the dog was not neglected. She was fed, watered and walked, but as far as playful interaction goes, I suspect she was left puzzled and needy. What did she make of Tim's sudden and permanent absence? Was she grieving too, as the famous examples of dogs faithful to their owners for years after their death would suggest? There are no answers here. Muffin just did what the rest of us were trying to do: reassemble the shattered pieces of the family jigsaw, and carry on.

I do remember 2004 as a year of journeys. We travelled north to Newcastle and south to Essex to stay with our extended family and lick the collective wound. We also made a long car trip to the furthest tip of west County Cork in Ireland, a place beloved by me and to Tim, and where he specifically wanted some of his ashes scattered, over mountaintop and ocean. It was a kind of pilgrimage. For this journey, Muffin was left behind with her dogsitters. I suspect it may have been a relief to the dog to be away from the dark atmosphere of the house. Children are known to blame themselves for all the bad things that happen in life – illness, death, divorce. It seems probable that dogs may do the same, in their eagerness to please, their limited cognition as to their own culpability and their acute emotional antennae, without the means to explain it all away. So I am glad Muffin got a holiday away from us, time to kick up her paws and run free for a while. She richly deserved it.

Like dogs, children must play. It is part of their job description. Children en masse – in the school playground, or down at the park by the swings – play particularly hard and loud. Always a reluctant schoolgirl, Molly found it painful to go back into the classroom after her father's death, into all that noise and bustle and ordinariness. After all, what had happened to her was exceptional, and was shrouded in deep silence, full of the darkest knowing. There was never any question, however, of other children making it difficult. Her closest friends showed an astonishing maturity in the way they handled the situation. If we underestimate the emotional capacity of dogs, then how much more casually do we dismiss the rich expanses of a child's heart. Molly's teacher, too, was gentle and determined. He told the class what had happened, and then they all carried on with the normal routine – no false piety, no avoidance or adult awkwardness. Still there, as a comforting constant, were the urgent imperatives of reading, writing, arithmetic and, the most essential ingredient, playtime.

Into this cheerful primary school jungle stepped Muffin, twice a day, to deliver and to collect her eleven-year-old charge. I went too, but I am sure she could have done it just as efficiently without me. Trotting in the reliable paw prints of her predecessor and good-dog prototype, Sandy, who still stood at the school gates like a seasoned campaigner, Muffin absolutely adored going to school. Sandy's owner Maggie says that she regards Sandy as a kind of dog ambassador, so impeccable in her behaviour that even the most timorous tiny child was won over by her charms. I feel the same way about Muffin.

The RSPCA had warned us that she might be nervous, even snappy, around young children, but nothing could be further from the truth. In fact, the only time Muffin has ever snapped at anyone's heels – apart from the occasional obligatory lunge at a passing postman – was when my Newcastle nephew Tom was in the teenage habit of rolling home at some late and ungodly hour after a night on the town. Muffin clearly saw herself, at her sentinel's post by the front door, as some kind of time-keeper and moral arbiter, and this behaviour she found beyond the pale. By the time Molly was old enough to indulge in the same thing, Muffin, like a worn-out mother with too many children, was too old and exhausted to care!

Tom is a rugby-playing, square-shouldered hulk of a guy. Like David and Goliath in the Bible – with Muffin taking on the role of David – she only ever picks on those at least five times her size (the same is true with dogs in the wood, which has led to some hair-raising near escapes down the years). As for babies and young children, she is decidedly motherly. She stands patiently while they ruffle her feathers and pull at her tail, and submits to being yanked along by her lead, up and down, up and down, in merciless repetition, with a kind and patient air. It was always with a happy spring in her step that Muffin would cross the playground on her daily commute, in order to greet the squealing hoards of kids just released from their tiny cramped classrooms into the bright afternoon air.

It was never easy getting Molly up and out in the morning – she is a night person like her father and, anyway, she didn't want to be at school – but Muffin came in handy here too. It was clear that the dog needed walking, and her enthusiasm to go out, her joyful, exploring spirit towards everything she saw, was an infectious thing.

There were two routes that we could take to school, and on each journey were landmarks that I remember with affection and nostalgia. We lived at the top of a hill, so the first part of the walk was always downwards, sharply, to the main Roundhay Road, passing a beautiful garden along the way, where the masses of opium poppies, come May, were so bright and huge in their scarlet coats that they dazzled and amazed. Once across the road, it was up the steep, steep hill on the other side, pausing to talk to the chatty cat called Vera, who cheerfully ignored Muffin's attempts to chase her off and followed us along the road, miaowing constantly with the latest gossip and weaving her immense black body round and round our legs. At the next corner house, an elderly gentleman sat in the window, eating his breakfast and reading his morning paper. We set our clock by him. If he had already finished, we were late for school.

Sometimes we called for Molly's friend Ellen, and this took us along Roundhay Road for several blocks, where the mass daffodil plantings all along the verge towards the park greeted us every spring. As we turned and walked up the hill to Ellen's house, we passed an old deserted mansion house, where a tramp, well known in the neighbourhood, used to shelter for the night, and where the tangle of overgrown shrubs loomed as in a fairy tale, shielding a sleeping princess. A hundred years' worth of imagining lay in those walls, behind those gates, and there was a local uproar when the council said the house was going to be demolished. It is still there, nine years on, and still full of empty dreams.

When the season turned, the cherry trees all along the banks of the road in which the school stood – our last road to cross – were loaded with blossom, pink and white. In conker season, the competition amongst the collecting children was cut-throat. It was all as if from a picture book of years gone by, these special and timeless childhood habits and meanderings. And at the centre of the action was our small dog, sniffing and skipping alongside her young companions. Sometimes, when it rained, or Molly pleaded tiredness, or showed a reluctance too entrenched to overthrow, we travelled the mile or so to school by car. It was not the same at all. The day needed the tread of our footprints over concrete and grass to give it meaning, to give us substance and purpose – and strength – in the long days of grief and recovery that had to be endured.

The earth is pushing up golden crocuses and tight-budded daffodils – signals of hope. There are days when the sun, pale and far away, sends messages of the coming warmth of summer, and I coax the old dog out into the garden for a spell of preparatory sunbathing. She still has enough sense to pick her spot with care, lying with a silly half smile in a watery shaft of light on the bleached-out lawn. She even managed a jubilant back roll recently, wriggling arthritically with her paws dangling awkwardly in the air, a hint of youthful memories passing briefly across her face. True, she did end up rather unceremoniously wedged in the flower border, between the cherry tree and miniature buddleia, but, never mind, the spirit was willing.

Encouraged by this, I decide to drive her to the wood for a short wander about in her old haunt. It is barely 200 yards down the road, but even that short stretch is beyond her now. She seems pleased to be here. Progress is slow, but she finds plenty of ravishing scent trails to follow and gets her nose down for a good, hard sniff. At home, it is only herself she can smell in the garden, plus a couple of neighbourhood cats. Here, in the wood, there are the fragrances of a thousand dogs to titillate her senses: some of them Muffin's old and departed friends; some of them new kids on the block, and therefore doubly intriguing. We make it up the short path to Tim's holly tree and back. The leaf formations for a million native bluebells are poking up, dark green and star-shaped. Muffin wanders amongst them and helpfully waters a few as she passes.

An elderly gentleman, with a beautiful face like creased leather, comes in through the green gateway as we go out. In front of him dances a young Border collie, weaving endless circles as she goes past and cracking a huge grin of delight at being out in the fresh air. The man pauses to put a hand on Muffin's back. He recognises a fellow sufferer. 'Oh, you're like me, aren't you?' he sympathises. 'I have arthritis of the spine. It's hard getting old, isn't it?' Muffin seems to have this effect on people. My mother-in-law is only half joking when, listening to my catalogue of Muffin's woes, she says, 'I have so much in common with that dog. I know just how she feels.'

There is a special sort of affinity between animals and the disenfranchised. It would be hard to imagine a dog, other than a special working breed, in the City of London, amongst the bankers, or in Parliament, with all the braying MPs. Ambition in animals is of a quieter texture and hue altogether. Put a dog in the middle of a pack of playful children, by the seat of a disabled person or at the bedside of a dying man, and it will be in its element, at home. A dog knows how to play. It understands suffering and pain, but status, money, fame? Forget it.

We take our leave of the lovely old man and his bouncy companion and head back to the car. I have to lift the dog in and out these days. She used to hate being handled like this, and would struggle and choke to get free. Now she surrenders gracefully and sinks like spilling water onto her smelly old duvet, stretched across the back seat. When she gets home, she falls into a deep and motionless sleep. You would think she had just conquered K2, which, in her own way, I suppose she had.

When Tim was in the last few months of his life, I took on a local allotment. The project was an impossible one. My plot was entirely covered with couch grass and invasive weeds of every possible persuasion. It was heavy clay and impenetrable to spade or trowel. At the top end was a magnificent and dilapidated old shed, which looked as if it had been there since the Middle Ages, and just below it stood a tiny pond, which was filled with frogspawn every February. The frogspawn reminded me of my mother, who had been a keen, though rather slapdash gardener.

All through my childhood, I watched her hurling clods of earth around, working off her phenomenal bouts of temper with her trees and bushes and bulbs and seeds. She found family life – three kids, a messy dog and an old-fashioned husband, who never did a stroke of housework in eighty-six years – unbearably frustrating. She took out her rage on the garden. In return, the garden grew, with a lusty zeal equal to all of her excessive emotions.

In spring, it positively shouted with joy: irises, daffodils, tulips and hyacinth; in summer, clematis, honeysuckle and roses. Such was her profligacy that the towering hollyhocks in her front garden could be seen, self-seeded and replicated, all the way down Cressing Road, in neighbouring front gardens. Mother's plants, like Mother herself, were indomitable. After working outside for hours on end, cursing and sweating and smeared with muck, Mum would then collapse in a heap under the generous shade of the tamarisk, or the weeping willow, drink copious amounts of tea and then sleep.

I never saw the point of her labours. My brothers kicked hell out of the lawn with their football. Our dog wrecked the bushes in her endless ferreting for tennis balls and bones, and she dug up the borders to hide bits of treasure from any passing dogs. My dad refused Mum's pleas for fruit trees in his annual preferred ritual of runner beans and potatoes. And she never got her lifelong wish for a pond, although in the end she dug her own miniature version, with a trowel and a bin liner, and, sure enough, the frogs came to visit, year after year, puddling about happily in the inch of muddy water she had created down by the old rockery. Mother had the Midas touch, and she presided with immense pride over her rough and ready outdoor queendom, but she did not pass the gardening bug on to her only daughter – not, that is, until I was in my late thirties.

I lived in a top-floor flat in London for ten years. I never missed the green, as a born-again city girl. But when Tim became ill with cancer, I discovered a new compulsion to grow things. When I was forty and we moved to Leeds, I got my own little garden for the first time. At last I realised what all the fuss was about. However much progress women have made in their working lives, the domestic domain is often still a source of drudgery and oppression. Housework is invisible, cooking and washing-up an endless round of repetition, but out in the garden there is a sense of freedom and creativity.

'Whatever you do,' my mum used to tell me, 'make sure you have a good view outside your kitchen window, because you'll spend a lot of time looking at it.' Prophetic words. I took care to plant big pots of honeysuckle and hops to grow up the back trellis at our first house in Leeds. Where we live now, there is a busy birdbath. There is nothing more hilarious than watching the resident family of sparrows dive-bombing each other in their greed for the morning seeds. There is a honeysuckle, with its potent memories of childhood, and a view over the entire green urban space. It is a sight I never cease to relish.

If you have a dog, it really helps to have a garden. Dogs are domestic creatures, and capable of being indoors for much of their day, but there is still a hint of wolf in them, and they need the fresh air, the wind and the rain – and room to stretch out in. When the RSPCA visited us to assess our suitability as dog adoptees, they eyed the garden keenly. It was small but secure. There was a good length for ball games on the wide sloping drive outside the back door, and space to sprawl on the little front lawn. The concrete made a useful bouncing place for tennis balls, and Muffin liked nothing more, as a young dog, than hurling herself wildly into the air to catch the high-flying missiles with a triumphant SNAP! of her jaws and an aerodynamic leap from her powerful haunches.

It was in this first garden that Muffin became my constant companion. Both husband and daughter preferred to be indoors most of the time, but Muffin was outside, like me, at the drop of a hat. She has never, in her long life, quite overcome her early experience of incarceration in a high-rise flat. To be outside is heaven to her. I was never particularly conscious of her presence, as I dug and planted, but she was just there, close to my feet, head on paws, snoozing or sniffing around, occasionally chewing at a ball, stick or toy.

'Where's your shadow?' a fellow parent once asked me, outside the school gates. It was one of the rare occasions when I had not brought the dog with me. Although her primary (self-elected) duty was to Tim when he became too ill to come outside, after he had died Muffin reattached herself to me with utter dedication. Almost without me realising it, she became my playmate and protector. She was well behaved too. In the garden, she was trained to take care. There was no trampling of the borders, or digging the newly turned soil. She observed perfect gardening etiquette, keeping to the paths and grass, and never, ever making a toilet of our little patch of paradise.

Gardening was like psychotherapy to me, without the words and the awkward silences. Maybe it was the same for the dog. In 2003, it became clear that there would be no summer holiday, because Tim was far too ill to travel, so when I saw the advert about local plots of land available to rent, I jumped at the chance. A summer project! It would be something to take our mind off the obvious slow decline in Tim's vitality. From the very first visit to inspect the site, Muffin came too, her tail waving like a triumphant flag as she took the lead up the stony path to our putative plot.

Urban allotments are like oases of calm hidden in unlikely places – behind high-rise tenements, near municipal sports centres and next to main roads. They look scruffy, unremarkable, even dull, but something magical happens the minute you enter the site. It is as if you have stepped through a Narnian wardrobe door, straight into the middle of the countryside. The atmosphere is more still, the birdsong more apparent, the air (so long as there has not been a recent delivery of manure) fresher and dense with fragrance. I have visited allotments in inner-city London, as well as on the outskirts of Leeds and in suburban Essex, and it has always been the same transporting experience. The dimensions of time and space are entirely altered. An allotment is like an island: and when you stand on it, you can be queen.

I fell in love with my plot immediately – a *coup de foudre*. It was the shed. It was the pond. It was the fact that it lay at the furthest, wildest end of the site, with a fine big hedge at its bottom perimeter, the houses of the nearby street out of sight behind. Everything about the place was calling out for our presence. Tim, very shaky on his legs by this time, had managed to join me on our initial visit, and his delight with the place was as evident as mine. We signed up on the spot. The dog wandered through the clumps of grass as if this was now her new second home, which it turned out to be over the next seven years. Some things cannot be avoided: illness, death, bereavement. But in the presence of loss, little triumphs are possible. Gardens – the way they die away in winter and bloom again in spring – are a self-renewing miracle. They create loveliness where there was just bare earth and weeds. Making the space beautiful, in my own garden and now on this old, tired allotment, became the project that gave me back my happiness and my hope. And Muffin was in on it from the start, a co-conspirator in paradise.

*

Everything – mind, body, heart – falls apart when someone you love dies, like a proud house crumbling to dust. Forget the brave words grieving people may tell you. It is much like childbirth in that respect: people lie, to protect their listener, and themselves. But the truth is stark. The truth is a deep, dark hole, beyond explicable emotion.

The thing that shocked and surprised me most about my own grief was that it was profoundly physical. My legs were dead as lead, my chest crushed with a heavy, immovable weight. It was all I could do to totter to school and back, to keep the bare bones of routine going, thanks to my daughter, thanks to my dog. And that is the way forward, of course: children, pets, friends, family, life itself still needs you. The kernel of future happiness lies there too: not in self-absorption, but in other people.

When I talked to a dear friend about the miseries of getting older, in another context, a long time after this, he said something telling. 'I don't care about ambition any more, about getting on, and me, me, me. I just want to be *useful*.' When we are wallowing in the mud, it is a helpful thing to remember.

After Tim died in January 2004, I feel as if I sleepwalked through the rest of the year. The garden went unweeded, and the newly acquired allotment was ignored. But by the beginning of 2005, I was ready to go back to earth. In the miserable cold days of January – maybe as a tribute to Tim's anniversary, maybe as a way of getting through it – I started to dig. Soon it was a kind of mania. However bad the weather – and Yorkshire weather can be truly vile – I packed up my kit and drove the two miles to the allotment and worked and worked. The dog, of course, came too, lying close by me as I wrestled with the earth, eager to make something grow from an unpromising patch of land and a gloomy situation.

One day I decided to transplant a little tree from my front garden to the top corner of the allotment. This was Tim's Corner, where he had sat in the hot sun, on his first visit, and was now to be a small, rough memorial to him. By the time I arrived at the site, the rain had started to fall. Soon it was coming down in sheets, with wind driving it slantways into my face. There was even the occasional sting of sleet, but I would not give up. I was determined to get that tree into the ground – even if the planting hole filled up with muddy water as fast as I dug, even if my hair and my clothes clung heavy to my skin and even if the dog soon disappeared to the shelter of the shed, with a look on her face of pity and utter incredulity mixed. She almost never went under cover unless I made her, being such a fan of freedom and the open air, but the weather on this occasion defeated even her.

Grief makes us do odd things. It drives us close to sharp edges and steep drops. I am just glad that the allotment, with its obvious symbolism of wild territory waiting to be tamed, was available as a resource upon which to vent my fury. I am gladder still that I had a canine companion to keep me company in an otherwise solitary endeavour.

Oddly enough, winter was a favourite time for me on the allotment. Muffin enjoyed it then too – no rival dogs to cramp her style, no suspicious plot holders eyeing her nervously as she romped innocently down the muddy paths between the different strips of land, careering through puddles and pausing only to sniff the huge and magnificently smelly mounds of manure, delivered by a local farmer and deposited on a neighbouring fallow plot, before continuing speedily on her way.

The whole place, out of season, was bleak, bare, deserted. There was something majestic in the desolation: naked brown earth and beaten-down grass tracks; all the different sheds, their cracked windows like old eyes, following you everywhere, monitoring your solitary moves; piles of wood and ancient rusting wheelbarrows. Here and there were winter crops: cabbages, broccoli, spinach and kale. But, generally, the territory was barren and I found that strangely consoling. It offered no false sympathy, and it matched my mood. Best of all, I was often the only person up there. I would sit in the shed with my flask of coffee, perched on the one fold-up chair and leaning on the table made out of an old kitchen door, and stare out of the latticed window, my mind drifting, like the winter seagulls, across land and sky. Solitude (the dog notwithstanding) has so many compensations. And sheds, like caravans, give the sense of living rough, whilst offering shelter and a minimum of warmth. I was around only during the daytime, unlike a fellow plot holder, who, as an insomniac and inveterate night bird, would often walk down from his nearby flat and sit in utter darkness, smoking his roll-ups, drinking his whiskey and watching the creatures of the night, most particularly the foxes, as they hunted and played. I always knew if the foxes had been – they scattered my carefully laid driftwood and pebbles and left piles of pondweed drooped over nearby borders. But I never, like my neighbour, dared go down at midnight to catch the creatures in the act. I always wish I had.

My allotment was in a pretty rough part of town. The nearby council estate was once dubbed the worst in Europe, although I used to live near South London's Stockwell Park Estate, and that comes close. You could regularly hear police sirens wailing through the neighbourhood streets, and there was the inevitable background thump of somebody's drum and bass on stereo or car radio. We were broken into, on the site, with tedious regularity. Those gardeners foolish enough to leave power tools in their sheds did so only once. 'In my day, it was scrumping for apples,' said the allotment secretary. 'Now it's top-end electrical goods or nothing.' The damage was rarely malicious, merely opportunistic. The lovingly tended rows of beans and potatoes, the soft-fruit bushes and plum and apple trees were usually left alone.

Spring was always a busy time. People started showing up as soon as the weather improved. By Easter, there was a frenzy of digging, sowing and planting. Gardeners worked side by side in companionable silence, pausing occasionally to lean on their spades in time-honoured fashion, and have a friendly, inconsequential chat, or just stare into the middle distance, waiting for their backs to stop complaining. Some of the happiest times of my life were spent sitting on my shed step, watching dragonflies glide over the top of the pond, and enjoying the gradual emergence of flowers over my makeshift arch, and broad beans, peas and frilly-edged lettuces in my little raised beds. Like dogs, gardens don't answer back. Like dogs, they speak volumes without ever uttering a word.

Muffin adored the allotment right from the start. As soon as I started assembling my gear at home – trug, secateurs, spade, gardening gloves, seeds – she would be dancing up and down the hall in anticipation. On the rare occasions that I did not take her with me, she would return to her basket with a despondent air, resigned to a morning alone indoors, but that didn't happen often. Muffin was my steadfast horticultural companion.

Molly, after a brief show of enthusiasm, right at the beginning, soon lapsed into teenage indifference and rarely came to the allotment, unless bribed to pick blackberries with her friend. That was fine by me. It was, after all, my great escape. Domestic duties, including those of motherly chores and family slave, definitely did not apply.

Many allotments have a rule about keeping dogs on the lead. For all I know, our allotment did too, but there was no question of that with Muffin. She always roamed free when we were there. It was her escape, as well as mine. Sometimes I would look at the high-rise flats nearby and remember that Muffin spent the first three years of her life cooped up in one of them, twenty-four/seven. She was now nearly nine, but still had catching up to do.

There was a main track that led from the entrance all the way to the far end of the site, where our plot was. When we arrived, winter or summer, Muffin would charge up this miniature road in a blur of fast, happy paws, with a manically waving tail. 'Here I am folks! Let's get this party started!' She knew exactly where to stop and turn sharp right, up a narrower lane, to our shed. If our nocturnal neighbour – a dog lover and particular fan of Muffin – was around, she would carry on up the path to say hello to him, before trotting back to me and choosing her spot for a good sniff, followed by a long lie-down, punctuated, perhaps, by several jubilant back rolls in dirt or grass.

She would always find her place with care. In spring, somewhere close to the pond and the shed was a favourite. But when summer arrived, and the sun beat mercilessly on the more exposed ground, she would wander down the hill and lie in the long, cool grass near the makeshift compost heap. In the summer months, the growth was so wild and opulent – a heavenly tangle of sweetpea, jasmine, honeysuckle and giant crocosmia, as well as the ever-rampant rough grasses and weeds – that she would disappear from view completely. It was a nightmare when I did the strimming. I had visions of decapitation, or an imprudent lopping of her lovely black tail, so I had to resort to shutting her in the shed, which did not please her one little bit.

Muffin considered herself Queen of the Plot. She never got bored, never wandered away to do unspeakable doggy mischief in the nearby thicket of trees, never pooed on other people's plots – well, rarely – and generally ingratiated herself shamelessly with everyone in sight. Trouble, when it came, was in the form of the secretary's dog, who had prior claim to the site, and never let Muffin forget it. And there was an awkward spell when a new, small, yappy dog arrived on a neighbouring plot, and pestered the life out of Muffin for a few weeks, before learning that our particular strip was out of bounds, and that Muffin was quite prepared to defend it with bared teeth and a lot of bad-tempered growling.

In general, nothing happened to spoil our perfect idyll. That changed for a few months in later years, when I took the rash step of joining the committee. I soon learned, and hastily resigned, falling back into grateful anonymity, and enjoying casual friendships again, rather than the accusing glances of plot holders, certain, as soon as I was on the committee, that I was 'the enemy', about to strip them of their rights and privileges and turf them off the site.

There is something about the exhaustion of spending the whole day outside with a contented canine companion that is deeply, beautifully healing. I know that I would not have felt nearly so free and determined to go off to the allotment at random times of the day, often the only person and certainly the only woman on that large and wildish piece of land, if I had not had Muffin at my side as a silent and watchful accomplice. My little dog spurred me on, in that, as in so many other things. She made me braver than I really am.

I am relying, not just on the old dog herself, but on my skilled and kindly vet to tell me when the game is up. Although much of me still shrinks from The Conversation – and despite sturdy vows to myself to avoid and desist – I am inevitably drawn to dog stories of all kinds these days – most particularly, descriptions of dog deaths – in the pursuit of a good end for Muffin.

Sometimes the information comes without prompting, as if I am wearing an invisible sign: 'My dog is very old. Please advise on a suitable course of action.' The bar manager at my local arts centre recently confided in me, unprompted, after an innocent inquiry as to how the woman was. Her old dog had been put down a couple of weeks previously. 'She was seventeen. She couldn't see; she couldn't hear. We used to totter down to the park together, but it was hard work. One morning I found her lying by the back door. She couldn't get up. She'd weed herself and was mortified. She was always such a clean dog. I made the decision there and then – and took her to the vet's the next day. The minute the needle went into her skin, she was gone. It's funny, she was always petrified of going to the vet and used to struggle like mad. But this time, she was perfectly calm, as if she was ready. Which is more than I was. I was a wreck. I really miss her. She used to lie at the bottom of the bed if I went for a rest during the day. When my hand dropped over the side of the mattress, I'd feel her nose push into it, followed by a gentle little lick with her tongue, as if she was saying, "Here I am. Still around." She was such a lovely dog.'

It was my turn to host a book group meeting last week. Muffin used to revel in this – a clutch of lively women, wine flowing freely, all making a huge fuss of her. She used to get right in the middle of the action in our small front room and beg shamelessly for food and attention. I would regularly have to boot her out, only to see her black nose pressed up against the glass-panelled door in the hallway, demanding re-entry. This time, however, she stayed curled up in her basket for the entire evening, oblivious to all the visitors, unaware of the occasion; any sense of social obligation, once so acute in her sensibilities, had disappeared without trace.

One of the group, Eileen, had a golden Labrador called Tess until a few years back, when she had to have her put down. I repeated my hopeful assertion that the vet would surely guide me on procedure when the end was near. 'But they won't,' she says. 'They won't do that. I kept expecting our vet to say something, but he never did. In the end, Tess couldn't walk, she was incontinent, she wouldn't eat or drink. I used to put water in my hand and try to get her to take a few drops, but she refused. Finally, the vet said, "I think she's trying to tell you something," and then we knew.'

Endings and beginnings. Another friend has just acquired a black Labrador puppy called Belle. She is keeping them awake at night with her crying. Like a new baby, she is insatiable and dominant in her demands. I am so glad she is here: young blood flowing wildly, just as the old blood falters in another's veins.

The most delightful thing about dogs is their sense of humour. Of course there are exceptions, as in the human world, but they are best avoided. Certainly all my favourite canines have had a glorious awareness of the art of being silly. After Tim died, the mood in the house was solemn and slow. Muffin took her cue from this for a while, but then gradually, as we humans started to emerge, she reintroduced a sense of fun into the proceedings. It was Molly who was her chief conspirator in this. If I provided the food and the action, Molly provided the frolics. Dressing up was the quickest way to get a laugh, and Muffin played to the gallery with consummate ease. For a nervous dog, who did not like being handled overmuch, Muffin was also rather a sensual creature, when approached in the right way.

These days, she jumps as if she has been stung when one of us goes to stroke her, but in her prime, she liked nothing better than being stroked and caressed all down the length of her narrow back, or under her chin and across her belly. A ritual began, after the evening meal, where Molly would sit on the floor, her long legs in a lazy diamond, and Muffin would lie in between them, snug as a well-fed bug, being tickled and talked to in the time-honoured nonsense manner that children and dogs know so well.

Muffin would let Molly do anything with her – ever since the very first days, when Molly was the only one who could persuade her to lie in her basket and relax. As a result, liberties were taken. First, it was the hats: bobble hats, hats with flaps, summer bonnets, straw boaters, baseball caps the wrong way round, glittering princess crowns with veils, Rudolph antlers and Santa hats with bells. I never knew just how many styles of haberdashery we kept under one roof, which was all the more remarkable, since none of us would be seen dead wearing a hat, barring Tim, when he lost all his hair and needed protection from the cold. None of us, that is, except the dog. She loved it. She would sit, motionless, like a dignified duchess having her portrait painted, her black and tan nose accentuated in length, her cheekbones fashionably high, her eyes – those dark brown liquid pools – unswervingly serious and intent. She never once gave the game away, as photo after photo was taken, but there was no doubt about it: she got the joke.

After the hats there was a mercifully short experimental period with outfits, mostly shoes, scarves and shawls, but once a mini commando jacket, which had to be squeezed over her two front paws and Velcroed in. Taking one look at her, my niece threatened to call the RSPCA and get the dog taken into care, so we stopped at that. But the hats were a perennial feature.

Although Muffin always longed to play Barbie, that was strictly out of bounds. The accessories were simply too small, the placement of them too precise. But the craze for beanie toys was an auspicious one, because they were soft and squishy little creatures and seemed to like nothing better than being piled high onto an immobilised Muffin (her own version of 'How many people can you fit inside a Mini?'). The dolls would mould themselves to Muffin's contours in a most agreeable fashion. Sometimes you could hardly see the dog for the dolls. Amidst it all, Muffin sat, serene and seraphic. She was absolutely in her element – the centre of attention – with Molly, her best human playmate, at her side.

People who have dogs seem to divide sharply into two camps where one thing is concerned: voices. There are those who invent an alter ego for the hapless pet – literally putting words into the dog's mouth – and those who most definitely do not. I once made the mistake of talking in Muffin's voice when my brother was staying. Since he was a dog owner himself, I assumed he would get the joke – far from it. He looked at me, appalled. 'What are you *doing*?' I quickly backtracked. After that, the dog was always silent when visitors were around.

The tradition of throwing voices began with my dear friend Liz, as most of my dog traditions do. She grew up in a houseful of dogs and, as a sensitive child and a skilful comedic actress, she invented voices for each of these dogs. Complete characters emerged, with particular quirks and prejudices, speech impediments, facial tics and regional accents, all specifically tailored to the dogs they animated. When I shared a flat with her in London, the voices emerged in all their glory, giving life – and fight – to dogs long gone that I had never met.

The greatest one of all was Martha, an Old English sheepdog. Martha was, to put it mildly, a roguish troublemaker of a character. She caused mayhem amongst the mildest of company – or, at least, the voice behind her did (Liz). Martha had the habit of finding someone's weak spot and then poking her paw right in it and pressing hard. Bear in mind that the dog herself had been dead for years. This was her restless, stalking spirit pacing the land! Arguments would start at dinner parties she attended. Harmonious foreign holidays with lovers and friends would turn sour when Martha turned up with her suitcase. Relationships were threatened. Something started in jest grew serious and deadly. One woman was so infuriated by Martha's sly interjections that she stopped the car she was driving with Liz, halfway up a tropical hillside, threw the door open and stomped off into the midday sun. 'That's it. I've had it with that damned dog.'

The canine voice is by no means an innocent invention. Molly, surprisingly, for she was a dreamy and creative child, never had an imaginary friend. She did not need an invisible alter ego, on whose spectral head she could pour blame for misdeeds, or through whose lips she could say all the rude and naughty things she did not otherwise dare to say, because she had Muffin. Slowly, through the years, a Muffin voice emerged that was crackling with humour and character to match even the redoubtable Martha. Muffin soon trod, metaphorically speaking, in the huge and mucky paw prints of Liz's most infamous invention. To begin with, we all had a go at a voice for Muffin. Tim's was goofy and rather childlike. Mine was affable and broad. Molly's, from the start, was more sophisticated and hilarious – with more than a hint of spite. Her voice stayed the course when the weaker manifestations fell by the wayside.

Muffin, channelled through Molly's rich imagination, became a well-travelled raconteur, friend to the stars – particularly George Michael and Elton John – and Kylie Minogue's biggest fan and confidante. She travelled everywhere by magic carpet, turning up at the Oscars one minute and Cannes Film Festival the next. She enjoyed rancorous disputes with all her dog friends down the woods, had numerous liaisons with actors and bar-room singers, and was forever going to get her nails done, or to have a 'bit of Botox' on her face, washing down the trials of the day with an endless stream of revolting cocktails with equally revolting names.

Muffin, of course, has long threatened to write her memoirs. The title is already in place: *Paws for Dramatic Effect*. There is no place that she has not been to, no party that she has not graced, no tacky B-list movie star whom she has not dated and later betrayed. At the height of her vocal powers, Muffin harangued me from daybreak to sunset with her incessant demands, her blatant boasting, her utter egomania. I threatened to ban 'the voice' on a regular basis, but then, before I knew it, was engaged, yet again, in an animated discussion – rising to a full-blown argument – with a dog who was, in reality, lying under the dining-room table, fast asleep and oblivious.

An awful lot of psychic spillage got channelled into the invented Muffin, but, mainly, it was an endlessly diverting comic soap opera, being streamed live in our living room, day after ridiculous day. When Molly turned eighteen and the world out-side the house got far more interesting than that inside, I noticed that 'the voice' had suddenly stopped. Muffin was fourteen and her health was beginning to falter. She was old. The life of a jet-setting canine superstar clearly no longer fitted, and, as Molly told me later, she was getting used to the idea that Muffin would die. A kind of preparatory separation was taking place. The end of the voice was the end of a long and playful era. Muffin had grown old whilst Molly had grown up. The conversations that took place now were strictly human, distinctly adult. I never thought I would miss that mischievous, trouble-causing, mother-baiting alter ego, but I really do.

One of the dog's greatest gifts to its human companions is the ability to channel emotion. The combination of a natural warm-heartedness and a helpful, sympathetic quality, makes dogs especially soothing to be around in the wake of chaos and distress. Muffin – except when she is wearing hats and having her photograph taken – is not self-centred at all. As long as she is fed, watered and walked, her demands are few. Her emotional palette with regard to her own feelings is limited in colours: she used to do happy and vivacious, now she does gloomy and confused. Despite this – or maybe because of it – she has always had highly attuned radar for the distress of others. She could, in her prime, get out of her own way, with speed and efficiency, in order to come to the aid of someone in trouble. Her influence was genuinely calming and resolving.

Muffin was never much good at the practical things – raising the alarm if someone fell unconscious or went into a fit would not have been her forte – but her emotional intuition was subtly attuned and impressive. Directly after Tim's death, this ability was seriously put to the test. Neither my daughter nor I is noisy in our sorrows; we prefer to cry in private. The suffering is discreet, but no less profound or overwhelming.

Whenever I wept for Tim, I tried to do it alone. There is only so much grief a child needs to witness, beyond the obvious shared experiences of illness, death, a mighty funeral and its aftermath. If a flood of emotion threatened to overcome me, I would take myself behind a closed door and wait for the sobs to subside. When I was recovered enough to open the door, Muffin was always there.

She got herself as close as she possibly could to the person in trouble. If the door was closed, she lay across the threshold and waited. If access was clear, she would move, swiftly and silently, to sit by my feet. She could hear a choke in the voice, a stifled cry, no matter how quiet, from wherever in the house she happened to be, and she was there in an instant. Often, she even anticipated the outburst, and offered herself in advance, before the person even knew what was about to break.

All she did was make herself present, in the softest and least demanding way. She would sit, or lie down – and stay there. She might offer a modest lick of the hand, but that was all. The most useful thing she could do – and she knew this instinctively, from the depths of her being – was just to turn up, and to remain, a true companion. If I looked at her face during these moments with Molly, or with myself, I saw a tenderness and an honesty that is so often lacking in our human faces, as we struggle to gain control, to keep ourselves strong and together. Dogs have no time for dissembling, no false pride. Their only mission is to be of use. Muffin, with her constancy and quiet devotion, in the early days after Tim's death, was more helpful than she would ever know or dream of. What she did was as natural to her as breathing, but the gift of it, in its simple beauty and grace, will never leave me.

There is a blind woman who comes to the singing group I belong to. She has a big-boned, beautiful Alsatian for a guide dog. The dog is always beside her, except when instructed otherwise. When tea break comes and Anna walks to the kitchen for her brew, the dog remains by the empty chair, but her eyes never leave Anna: she tracks her, watches her, wherever she goes. She is a working dog, and this is her job – to be her owner's eyes, to see everything Anna cannot know – but there is so much more to it than work. The dog is clearly devoted to her owner, and to witness this is a privilege. On the first night they came, the dog was perplexed when everyone stood up and sang. Her pointed ears stood up a little more sharply, there was a wrinkle in her brow, but she took it all in her stride.

In the ten years I have been singing – another survival strategy learned when Tim was very ill, and a source of continuing joy now he is gone – I have brought Muffin along only once. It was Bonfire Night and she was too frightened to be left on her own. That night a loud and jolly Afro-Caribbean guy was leading us. He was particularly bouncy, and wanted us all to dance, stamp our feet and clap hands, as well as sing rather loudly. But my dog has a jealous and puritanical streak. She hates it when people embrace – pushing herself in between them like some canine Victorian chaperone – and she will not tolerate dancing.

She jumps up, she barks, and she carries on doing so until the source of her annoyance ceases. So when our choir leader demonstrated each song, clapping his hands and beating time with his feet, Muffin joined in. She gave voice and she ran at him, jumping up and down, the second he opened his mouth. It was as if she had been specially trained to attack and silence him – the only black man in the room – my dog the bigot. Nothing she has done has embarrassed me more. We left early so that she could shout at the fireworks instead.

Noisy events have never suited Muffin, although she does like a big gathering, which seems to remind her of the wild pack she grew up with, and the sheer weight of numbers soothes her. But silence is her favourite sound, which makes her the perfect dog for me. For the past decade, I have been exploring the paths of meditation. In part, this is a reaction to the ten years on cancer wards, under threat of illness and death, when my brain was in constant overdrive, with a never-ending stream of words, recriminations and questions, day and night. I needed to find a way to stop the mental torture.

I am trained in dance, and during a particularly gruelling ballet class in 1986, I injured my sacroiliac joint. At times of acute or continued stress, whether physical or emotional, the injury recurs and my lower back seizes up, rendering me immobile, my body in a state of remembered shock. In 2001, the year when Tim's decline was most extreme, my back was in a mess. I turned to the Alexander technique, a system of psycho-physical realignment, which unlocks bad postural habits and encourages a new and freer way of being. It worked like a charm. One of the most treasured exercises in the technique is to lie semi-supine, knees bent up, feet flat to the floor, head supported by books, back lengthening and widening along the ground. I love this position. So does the dog.

There is a perfect place to lie down in the back room by the radiator. Muffin got to know when I was headed in that direction and there would be an unseemly scramble as we fought for the prime spot in the quiet and the warm. Once she was booted out – because she always got there first – she would take up position on the other side of me, and we would both enter an extended Zen-like state of soporific calm. Sometimes we were there for up to an hour, deaf to the world's demands, side by side, utterly immobile, utterly content. Then, when it was time to move, Muffin would demonstrate an impeccable back stretch, spine lengthening in a supple and superb curving action, which put my own lumbering human ascent rather to shame.

My dog the yogi. My dog the Buddhist monk. I never would have believed that a dog could meditate, but Muffin became a genuine adept. I always meditate in a special corner of my bedroom. It is a very small space and Muffin never comes there now – she is too old and creaky – but for years she would bound upstairs at the sound of the bowl chiming, as if primed by a sacred alarm, a call to canine contemplation. When I knelt down, she would take her place behind me and lie down quietly. Sometimes her eyes would close; sometimes they stayed open, with a far-away look in them, which was, in itself, deeply restful.

She hated loud singing but loved it when I used to chant, a rhythmic repetition of the Dalai Lama's call to compassion. Clearly the dog approved. It is hard to quantify what she did when she lay beside me. There was a texture and a depth to her presence, that is all I can say. This was perhaps the dog's favourite role of all: being an accompanying spirit, with a deep sense of balance and calm, offering the one thing she always shared with unstinting generosity – a sense of solace and of peace.

Chapter Five

Woods and Water

Spring has blossomed beautifully, if briefly, this year. After a cool start, March 2012 has simply blazed with colour and heat. And the old dog is still with us. It is good to give her some warmth and fresh air, out in the back garden, after a mild but interminably dark winter. She may have lost much of her sensual connection to the world around her, but this she can still do with aplomb: sunbathe. There is something almost feline about Muffin when she lies in the sun. Other dogs I know, particularly the ones with thick, heavy fur, quickly take shelter from the heat – not Muffin. She will lie for far too long, panting like a steam engine, luxuriating in the wonderful muscle-melt that only comes with the deep, penetrating fire of the sun.

Her method of lying down is eccentric and awkward these days, since the arthritis has penetrated her lower spine. When indoors, she stands and sways for a long, long time, as if plucking up the courage – as indeed she may be, for the manoeuvre is undoubtedly unpleasant – to get down to the ground itself. It used to be her haunches, powerful and muscle-coiled, that got her up and down. Now the front legs and shoulders have taken over. When she does make it down – her front legs splayed wide, her back legs tucked up awkwardly beneath her bum – she looks like a little spatchcock chicken, ready to roast. But out in the sun, she seems simply to pour herself into the ground, and once she is there, the basking is prolonged and lovely.

We do not go far these days. Muffin has gone into a kind of Howard Hughes seclusion and her public appearances are rare. We did have a long-standing arrangement to stay near the East Yorkshire coast at Filey to celebrate a sixtieth birthday in the family, and I was keen to honour that. So, at the end of March, with the sun shining in its unhabitual profusion, the three of us set off – daughter, dog and me. Our accommodation was a converted barn, very tasteful and modern, with cream carpets and pale furnishings throughout. In short, it was a potential nightmare, since our dog has black moulting fur and an unpredictable pattern of digestion and expulsion, verging perilously on total meltdown, so I approached the event with increasing trepidation. But we did it, somehow, and suitable allowances were made. Everyone else in the party slept upstairs, with the jacuzzi bathrooms and en suite luxury. Muffin and I, meanwhile, were billeted in the remedial wing, in a small downstairs room, close to an outside door and a toilet with sink for emergency sluicing. It worked. There were no mishaps. Muffin crashed and banged her way around the house, with no obvious hurt to furnishings or animal, during the day, and I slept with one eye open at night.

One day we poured the dog into the car to go to Filey. The younger, fitter family members, including one unfeasibly bouncy and glamorous young dog, who made Muffin look like something from the Stone Age, scampered down to the beach. Muffin and I took a slo-o-o-w promenade along the top, where people of a certain age had amassed themselves on wooden benches to gaze at the water, flat as a millpond in the unusual calm, and enjoy the carefully manicured lawns and flowerbeds. It seemed like a place in suspended animation, where nothing real or remarkable had ever happened, nor ever would. So we fitted in quite well.

Muffin does look rather extraordinary when she moves these days. Her spine sinks low in the middle and she plods along reluctantly, or pauses long, head drooping, like those shaggy ponies you sometimes see hobbled at the side of the road, clinging to a piece of chewed-up, sterile earth. She has the face, grizzled and faded, of an Old Testament prophet – ancient Methuselah – miraculous, in her own way, and rather disturbing too.

As we meandered along the Filey seafront, a bald-headed man with no teeth shouted out, 'How old's yer dog?'

'Fifteen and a half,' I replied.

He nodded, pausing for a heartbeat. 'She's buggered, isn't she?' Despite the protestations of his female companion, who tried to soften the truth by claiming that Muffin was simply taking the sea air in a stately fashion, I had to agree with him.

Her obvious degeneration has upset people in the family who

haven't seen her for a few months. Then she seemed to function in a more or less normal way. Now, quite frankly, she would – were she human – be sedated and pushed around in a wheelchair to aid her mobility and stop her strange pacing repetitions, but she is a dog, so she presses on regardless.

Before we leave our holiday home, the relatives, each in their gentle, individual way, say goodbye to the old dog. It was good to take her with us, and she seemed to benefit in an indefinable way, but I think that is the last of the travelling now. Home is the safest place, the only place where she seems really to relax.

Despite a little collection of bought seashells, and some pebbles I stole from the strange remote beach at the bottom of Flamborough Head cliffs while Muffin slept up above in the car, I hardly feel that I have been to the sea at all. It is the first time ever that I have been to the coast with the dog and not come back utterly windblown and sprayburnt, both of us stinking gloriously of brine and shaking the damp sand out of our skin and fur for days to come. I feel cheated on her behalf, because the sea was once the wildest domain Muffin ever knew. She loved it with a passion and embraced its anarchic rhythms as if her heart would burst with joy. Those were the days; those really were the days.

When our daughter was small and we still lived in London, the beaches we visited on the south-east coast and in quiet Rye were child-friendly and suitably tame and sandy. Many a hole was dug, usually by Tim, and our one small child – squealing with delight – was buried, wriggling, inside. When Molly was four and we moved north, and once the dog arrived, the summer beach holiday became a thing of the past. Dogs are banned from the sand in high season and rightly so. The invigorating sea air and inadvertent slurpings of salt water loosen the canine bowels like little else. We started visiting the sea in the middle of winter, at Christmas and New Year, instead, taking flats and cottages that invariably welcomed 'one small, well-behaved dog'. Much of Yorkshire is open country still, and its inhabitants are natural dog owners, as are the letting agents, so Muffin always came along.

The coastline of North Yorkshire is spectacular. Lined with tiny fishing villages and rugged cliffs, vast expanses of heather-studded moorland opening out behind, the North Sea boils at the land's edge with a brilliant slicing fury. Winter, stripped as it is of every adornment, sees the land and ocean at its most bleak and beautiful. I have only vague memories of the first time Muffin visited the beach – I cannot recall the date or the exact place – but I do know she was ecstatic. She cared nothing for its beauty, but she loved the spaciousness, the utter wildness. And she did what she had done the very first time I released her from the lead as a newly adopted dog, in the Fairy Woods behind our house: she ran and ran and ran.

With the exception, perhaps, of a beautiful, bare-backed horse, on which to gallop through the surf, I can think of no finer companion to have by the sea than a dog. It is a rare canine that does not embrace the wanton freedom of the water's edge.

Certainly that was Muffin's initial and abiding response – joy.
The ocean is a huge and liberating place. The normal rules of
civilisation do not apply. People feel happy to dress and undress
in public (weather permitting) and engage in hardcore romping,
whether with a bucket and spade or with each other. The sea,
with its sucking, insistent rhythms and invisible mysteries, mir-
rors a consuming instinct inside us all: the drive towards death
versus the desperate urge to live.

Watching Muffin run on the beach, head thrown forwards,
lips stretched back over her sharp, sharp teeth, tail waving like
a pirate's flag in the wind, paws flailing, I could see both those
extremes embodied in her movement. If she could, she would
have run straight off a cliff edge and carried on running, into
thin air and the sky itself. Miraculous. On arrival at a new beach,
her disorientation kept her timid at first. There would be short
scampers and prolonged bouts of sniffing, growing progres-
sively bolder. And then she was off, into the full flight of circular
running and leaping, her body describing bigger and bigger
curves at breakneck speed, until finally she slowed, tongue
lolling, sides heaving, to a drunken amble amongst the rocks and
over the endless pebbles, on her own little trip to paradise and
back.

Other dogs might hurl themselves into the sea at this point,
having explored the beach to its full extent – not Muffin. The
most she would consider was a noisy splash in the surf of the
shallowest wave. Swimming was never a sport she favoured,
except *in extremis*. She was more of a sprinter, with the ground

safely beneath her paws. The only agony she ever suffered by
the sea was when any of us (usually Molly, who was far more
intrepid and hardy than either parent) decided to paddle deep or
swim. Then Muffin would hover nervously at the water's edge,
her rounding-up instinct fully to the fore, and wait for the mis-
creant to dock safely on dry land. Although she never barked or
howled, as my own childhood dog Tess had done, in her utter
misery that we might be drowned, and that she would be solely
to blame, Muffin's more muted, unexpressed anxiety was
nonetheless obvious and upsetting. Things were always better
for her when we were all safely on the beach and, preferably,
running like crazy to keep alongside her.

Only once did Muffin fall in the sea herself. As with all her
near-drownings (of which there have been at least four), it fell
to me to come to the rescue. In January 2001, we went to
Whitby for a holiday with friends. A few miles north of the
town is a tiny little fishing village called Staithes, which nestles,
like a well-guarded secret, at the bottom of a steep and daunting hill. Apart from a footbridge across the river estuary, from
one escarpment to another, and a stone pier jutting out from a
small, curving foreshore, there is not a great deal to explore.
The beach is tiny, with none of the wider expanses of the bigger
resorts like Whitby and Scarborough. Inevitably, we ended up
sampling the extent of our options by walking the full length of
the pier, carefully negotiating its flat, wet, stone surface, the tide
lapping, deep and freezing cold, on either side. Well, the
humans were careful; the dog was not. She found the slippery

walkway a bit of a lark, skipping backwards and forwards with a confidence verging on showing off. All was fine. Then, in a heartbeat, she was gone – straight off the side of the pier into the icy water.

For a split second, everyone froze. They gawped. No one moved. No one said anything. Before I knew it, I was gone too, up to my chest in the coldest water I have ever experienced or hope to experience again. I take my tea scalding hot, and my baths likewise, so the shock of it nearly killed me. But I am, like my dog, at the mercy of my reflexes when a crisis occurs. Before I know it, I act. It was, on reflection, deeply comic: Muffin floundering around like a baby whale, her blind, doggy paddle panic making her less and less easy to catch; me cursing and splashing about in her wake, and increasingly desperate, both to save the dog and to survive the intense cold. Somehow we got out, but the worst was yet to come: the walk, soaking wet, back up the high, impenetrable hill to the car.

My mood was unspeakably foul. I hated the dog and I hated the other humans, dry and snug in their big coats and fake fur hats. This rage was unappeased, even by the kind act of my friend Bev, who saw an unlikely little shop that was open and emerged bearing a pair of grey woollen tights, which, when I changed into them, only reached to mid-thigh and itched like the devil on damp flesh. My skin, when revealed, was mottled scarlet – in places almost blue – with the cold. My teeth would not stop chattering for nearly an hour. I didn't speak to the dog, herself pretty woebegone and salt-encrusted with the residue of one of Staithes' deepest and most unwelcoming harbour waves, for much, much longer than that.

I think, of the three of us in our small family unit, it was Tim who loved Muffin the most and vice versa. When she came along, he was already five years into his ten-year struggle with cancer. His illness was deep rooted, invasive and repressive. Already an exceptionally quiet man, his cancer had a profoundly inhibiting effect. Only two creatures found a way of unlocking his hidden vitality: his beloved daughter Molly, with whom he shared a matchless capacity for silliness, and his dog.

Psychoanalyst Clarissa Pinkola Estés has something interesting to say on the significance of this. 'Dogs,' she says, in her book *Women Who Run With the Wolves*, 'are the magicians of the universe. By their presence alone, they transform grumpy people into grinning people, sad people into less sad people; they engender relationship.' I saw this with my own eyes when I watched Tim and Muffin together. And their synchronised flow, one to the other, was never more apparent than by the sea. Something about the peace of the water, the rhythm of the tide, the spaciousness of sea, sand and sky, tuned them more fully into one another, and it made me glad.

At that point in our lives together, Muffin would have done anything for Tim, to the point of self-sacrifice, such was her devotion. Pinkola Estés would not be surprised at this either: 'Dogs represent, among other things, she who loves from the heart easily and long, who forgives effortlessly, who can run long, and fight, if necessary, to the death.'

Both Tim and I were gourmet sea lovers, eschewing the gaudier or tamer resorts of the Yorkshire coast for the bleaker bays and clifftop hideaways. We were particularly snobbish about Scarborough, with its stick-of-rock cheeriness, its hoards of noisy paddlers and fairgoers, and the lace-curtained, seaside hotels, Full English Breakfast Victoriana. We liked our sea adventures spiked with thunder and storm-threatening gloom. Scarborough out of season has one brilliant asset that fits this bill: the North Bay. Here the beach is a gorgeous expanse of blank sand to run on. When the tide is high and the weather rough, the waves roar over the esplanade with a ferocity that is breathtaking and madly beautiful.

At Easter 2002, a friend lent us her little house in a street not far from the North Cliff and Bay. Tim had just emerged from a particularly grim year of physical wastage and psychological depression. With his characteristic determination to bounce back and have another go at life – a trait I see strongly in Muffin as she approaches the end of her life – he looked forward to this seaside holiday with particular relish. It was cold that year, and the wind whips up a fair fury around the North Bay when the forecast is bad, so we dressed accordingly: fleeces, thick jeans, walking boots and gloves. Tim, by this time, was permanently bald – partly due to extensive chemotherapy and partly an alopecia from the prolonged stress of his cancer experiences – but at least he had a fine head for hats. The headgear of choice for the winter coast was either a fur hat with flaps or a baseball cap.

Muffin, of course, had modelled both of them in her time. Our photo albums are littered with grainy pictures of her wearing them, and of Tim and the dog on various beaches: him in one or other of the two hats, and the dog carrying, chasing or retrieving a whole string of soggy, sand-filled toys, because when man and dog left a house together, they were *never* without the tools of play. It was wonderful to watch Muffin fetch a ball on the beach, where no tree, house or road stood in her way, no pesky bouncing obscured it from view. With Tim's prodigious throwing technique sending the ball flying improbably high, she would run like the wind in pursuit of an object soon so far away we could hardly see it, but Muffin, with unerring instinct and accuracy, retrieved it every time. Better still, on the expansive Scarborough beach, was the arrival of the frisbee. I remember a large purple frisbee (followed by smaller replacements as the week went on) being Muffin's Easter present that particular year. From the straight line of the flying ball to the curving grace of the frisbee in flight, Muffin adjusted her technique with the poise and speed of a miniature ballerina. Her action was like a long, flowing line of poetry, quite mesmerising to watch. In the end, Muffin was almost delirious with fatigue. She bashed hell out of several frisbees in the space of one short holiday. Proceedings were only stopped – usually by me – when the dog's tongue bled from lacerations sustained as she took the fast-flying plastic straight into her mouth from thin air, snapping her jaws shut a little too keenly in order to make the catch.

Some people go to the mountains. Some people go to the sea. For me, it has always been the vast rhythms of the tide – something about the ever-changing mood, the fluidity and the underlying depth and constancy of the ocean – that holds me fast in times of trouble. I always assumed this was because I am British, an island girl from a nation of boat-builders, seafarers and fishermen. Then I spoke to a Hungarian woman and she said she felt exactly the same. She, too, longed for the sea, but her country is landlocked and beleaguered with troublesome nations on every border. With the exception of the glorious Lake Balaton and two big rivers, the Danube and the Tisza, it has no other expanse of water, and definitely no sea. Either country seems to call forth the same need. It is, after all, a matter of psychology, not nationhood. Irish poet Liz Mellon puts it clearly in her poem 'The Colour of Light':

If you wonder where you are
in the scheme of things
in your life, your only life,
go to the sea and the mountains
where constancy shifts
in the colour of light
and nothing is taken for granted.

How it is for dogs, I cannot say, but Muffin has always responded with enormous enthusiasm to the sea. She was there alongside us on beaches when Tim was alive, and there, too, when we went for coastal repair in the years following his death. These were precious days indeed, because once Molly became a teenager, the charms of the city took her over. Paris and London replaced Whitby and Staithes, and the dog was billeted out to long-suffering, canine-loving friends.

In 2005, Muffin was with us, on Whitby's magnificent west cliff, up the 199 steps to the wreckage of the Abbey and wind-battered St Mary's Church, on the anniversary of Tim's death, to honour his memory with a slug of whiskey and a salute. She was there the following year, 2006, in the summer, trotting off with Molly to the little beach by the landing stage where Dracula made his first entry onto British land, disguised – appropriately enough – as a large black dog. (Dogs lend themselves beautifully to symbolism of all kinds, especially that of depression and death, as well as loyalty and love.)

Invitations from family and friends were abundant at a time when we really needed them. For some of the more exotic or far-flung seaside places on offer – the Spanish coast and the south-west peninsula of Ireland's County Cork – Muffin could not come with us. I have always stopped short at the prospect of a dog passport. Air travel would kill her, and, given her propensity for jumping in out of her depth at every opportunity, the thought of a sea ferry, or boat travel of any kind, makes me quake. Putting her in a crate, heavily tranquillised for transportation, was not an option. But everywhere in this country her faithful shadow was omnipresent.

Just as our lives – Molly's and mine – started to expand and grow, out of the darkness of illness and death towards a more optimistic, light-filled horizon, so Muffin's own vitality seemed in the ascendance. By 2005, she was nine years old, by dog standards already a mature, even middle-aged dog, but you would not have thought so to look at her. Released from her duties as caring companion to her beloved master, and sensing a more optimistic atmosphere in the house – with a fresh start set in motion by the move to a new house in 2006 – Muffin really began to blossom. Despite her congenital heart defect, she continued to run at a phenomenal speed, her taste in toys to run after growing grander as she took flight.

When Molly was eleven or twelve, there was a retro craze for hula-hooping in the playground. Molly caught the bug and got super-efficient at the hip-snaking moves necessary to keep the hoop aloft. The only snag was that Muffin took a fancy to the hoop too. She kept trying to catch it – and wrecked Molly's record-breaking times in the process. In the end, there was only one possible solution: buy one each.

When friends invited us to stay on the Wirral, on England's north-west coast, and took us on a huge sandy beach for a wild and windy walk one day, we had to stop at the seaside shop and buy two new hoops – one for Molly and one for Muffin. The hula-hoop required a whole new approach, and one that Muffin perfected on this holiday to memorable effect.

First of all, the hoop had to be rolled rather than thrown. Once it was set in motion, and was snaking off on its own wide, curving pathway, the dog would give chase, galloping in full flight, then skidding to a halt as she took the thin plastic tube in her mouth. For the first few attempts, that was it: dog and hoop would collapse in an ungainly tangle. But it did not take Muffin long to find a way to keep running, by taking the nearest edge of the hoop in her mouth, then tossing her head backwards and flicking the whole contraption up and over, so that she was running in the centre of the circle, keeping the whole hoop aloft, like some demented circus dog in the middle of a carefully staged performance. The only things missing were a ruff and a cap of bells.

Like a holy fool, Muffin kept us laughing, running and romping through our endless seaside adventures down the years. She was the mascot of my daughter's childhood, the symbol of joy and freedom, the reminder that nothing is ever so serious that it cannot be transcended, if only momentarily, by the sound of the waves crashing in your ears, pebbles and sand beneath your feet, and a daft little dog trotting contentedly at your side.

All in all, Muffin's beach days were long and happy. Some dogs never see the sea in their whole lives. But for her it was like an old friend – at least when kept at paw's length, as she explored yet another rocky foreshore in the freezing winds and rains of a Yorkshire winter. Although the beach was beyond her by spring 2012, she was still game for it just a couple of months before. In January 2012, we rented a little cottage in Robin Hood's Bay – just south of Whitby, and a real smugglers' cove of a place. The approach down to the bay is vertiginous, as everywhere on the

North Yorkshire coast: it's all right going down, but murder going up. But if we took our time, Muffin, even in her dotage, managed it.

It had been a year or so since we had been by the sea. In that year, the dog's cognition had been greatly impaired by the stroke and encroaching blindness. Would she even remember the beach, derive any pleasure from the salt tang of the North Sea winds that used to whip her into such a frenzy? I woke early on our first morning there. The sun was still flushing the skies a pretty dawn pink when the dog and I tottered through the little back alleys to get to the sea. The tide was low. The dog was non-committal, head and tail down, as she followed obediently in my footsteps, at the end of her lead. Then we were there: down a concrete ramp and onto a rocky outcrop, the sand damp beneath us, and a big, indifferent sky over our heads. No one else was around and except for the gulls – silence.

There was no epiphany, but there was something, something so slight no one else would have noticed. But I did. The dog suddenly, briefly, lifted her head, did a barely perceptible double-take at the beach around her, sniffed the air, stood up to her ankles in a shallow pool, and looked at me, as if to say: 'Yes. I remember. This was the place.' And that was it. Robin Hood's Bay was the last time Molly and I took Muffin on a proper walk, up along the cliff edge to Boggle Hole and back by the water's edge to the pub for lunch, followed by a long, long sleep. And that was enough.

*

Very old dogs are similar to new babies. They have limbs like rubber dollies, eyes with a misty faraway look. They are like lovable aliens, with toilet habits that are both unpredictable and unsavoury, verging on the disgusting. They display a general air of incomprehension as to where they end and the rest of the world begins – no self, no other, just an amorphous mass, a warm, breathing, permanently dazed and bewildered existence. But where the breath of a baby is milky sweet, steer clear of the old dog's mouth, for pity's sake.

Muffin's breath these days is like a Parisian sewer – unbelievably foul – and strange things are starting to erupt from her fur. When my childhood dog Tess grew old, she too grew an alarming number of lumps, bumps and pustules, and became undoubtedly disfigured as age and ill health overtook her. Muffin stayed very pretty, well into her sixteenth year. Now, I must confess, the Era of the Gargoyle is being entered. Those eyes are no longer brown; they are a permanent cloud of grey. The nails on each of her four paws are immensely long – ridged, thick and curled back on themselves. If I were a good owner, I would get them clipped, but any trip to the vet these days provokes trauma and fatigue, in both the dog and me, beyond the bounds of cosmetic considerations. She can hang on to those claws: Crufts is hardly awaiting her entry form for Best in Show. She now also sports a kind of carbuncle or wart just above her eyebrow. It is very unsightly. I keep it clean and swabbed daily. It's not getting much better, but it's not getting worse. This is the current criteria: maintain the status quo and don't expect miracles –

don't expect anything any more. It astonishes me to find her still breathing by the morning. Everything else is a bonus.

I read a beautiful article by Gene Weingarten, in the *Washington Post*, about the joys of his old dog, now sadly dead, but so clearly loved throughout his life, and so eloquently remembered in Weingarten's writing, that it is hard to be too regretful. A good life, well lived. Weingarten salutes the capacity of the old dog for tranquillity and acceptance. 'Old dogs can be cloudy-eyed and grouchy, grey of muzzle, graceless of gait, odd of habit, hard of hearing, pimply, wheezy, lazy and lumpy. But to anyone who has ever known an old dog, these flaws are of little consequence. Old dogs are vulnerable. They show exorbitant gratitude and limitless trust. They are without artifice. They are funny in new and unexpected ways. But, above all, they seem at peace.'

I look at my own dog and wonder if she, too, is at peace. It is hard to believe so sometimes, when she is wandering aimlessly through the house, barging into furniture and bashing her poor self for the hundredth time that day. It is sad to see her struggle to locate the dish of food beneath her very nose, when she used to smell a tasty morsel from the other end of the house and come running in anticipation. Worst of all is when she gets stuck in a corner somewhere, and just stands there, unseeing, unhearing, for minutes on end, until someone finds her and steers her back to her basket.

When she finally surrenders and falls blissfully asleep, curled on her side in her basket, nose tucked under her paws, head pushed into the soft contours of her bed, body flopped in utter relaxation, then she really does look at ease, totally given into the rhythm of rest, and without any trace of the waking bewilderment that follows her through her days like a permanent spiteful shadow. I long for her eventual death to be like this, as it could not be for any of the people I have lost, though they so richly deserved it too. For this, surely, is the ultimate aim after a long life: a peaceful sleep, from which there is no more waking, but no more struggle either – a sort of doggy nirvana. That seems an appropriate final gift.

It is impossible to say which brought the dog most pleasure in her life: woods or water. Certainly she never was so fast or free as when she was chasing frisbees over miles of empty sands, but the beach required toys and chasing. There were only so many rocks she could sniff without realising that the smell was the same – salt, salt, salt, and lots of it. With woods and moors, the diversions were endless. The traces of animals and birds excited her nose. The trees and pathways honed her tracking skills, offered possibilities and mysteries hidden just around the corner. By the water, she revelled in the open skies; in the woods, she hid and played and enjoyed her animal secrets. Probably she was most herself, the least accessible to humans, and the most beautifully absorbed, when she was in a patch of forest, a meadow or on a moor. Then, she was truly in her element.

The first really wild space she saw was Ilkley Moor. She was still a very new and clueless dog – only two or three weeks out of the animal shelter, very thin and jumpy, with a haunted, abandoned look. A friend invited us on a cold birthday walk at the end of December, 1999. It had been raining and sleeting over the previous week and everywhere had the cold bitter dampness particular to a Yorkshire winter. Every region has its own version of weather. I cannot explain what makes the wet and cold in our region different from anywhere else, but when I breathe in, there it is, that specific Yorkshire tang!

There was no rain when we arrived, but a chill wind was blowing. Ilkley is a high, bony piece of land. When you climb to the tops, even on a warm, still summer's day, there is invariably something cool blowing around your nether regions. The walk up from the car park is steep and dramatic. The Cow and Calf – one massive 'mother' hulk of millstone grit, with a smaller, rounder offspring flung a little way off – guard the entrance to a remarkable rock amphitheatre, like a giant's cave with the roof blown off, the ground littered with stones and gathered pools of dank and freezing rainwater. The crazy people gather here: rock climbers and abseilers by day, frightening the life out of the casual tourists by swinging from the sheer heights with a cavalier glee; party people by night, consuming their cans and making various kinds of whoopee, leaving their prehistoric traces by carving lovers' names – and the occasional profanity – into the grey, long-suffering stones.

The day we visited, it was not this dark, rather sinister natural cathedral that interested us, but the moors above it – the great expanse of scrubland and sky. Tim loved the moors above everything. Whenever we drove to Whitby on the scary switchback road that leads up and over the headland to the coast, a contented silence would fall upon him. He never learned to drive, so he was free to stare out of the passenger window at the purple haze of heather stretching as far as the eye could see, a bleak and unforgiving canvas of nothing, broken only by the occasional sheep or fat black crow. Many of the Yorkshire men I know have a particular craggy aspect – poet Ted Hughes the most famous example. They seem to have rocks and cliff edges built into their faces, written in their bones. Tim was actually fine featured, with long and almost delicate fingers, but he was a big man – a mountain of a person from a tough, rocky region. Little Muffin could not have been more different, with her slender paws, her thin, small frame and her dark Hispanic looks, but she, too, would find her place in the wilder corners of her Yorkshire home. The beautiful iron entered her soul too.

December 1999 on Ilkley Moor was Muffin's first exposure to such a huge open space. I had only just started letting her off the lead round the back of our house, so Ilkley was a much scarier proposition. Can dogs feel awestruck? If so, then Muffin did that day. The terrain was rough. There were well-trodden pathways, leading ever upwards, ever further away into the distance, but as soon as you left them, the landscape turned treacherous and full of secrets. What looked to be solid scrub was actually marshy and soft: hidden pools formed by the recent rains snaring the unwary walker, sending water over the top of hiking boots, through thick socks and onto cold and complaining toes. Muffin was soaked within minutes.

I kept her on the lead to start with, but after a while decided to let her run free. And run she did, but in a raw and random fashion, very different from the easy focus she would find on beaches and in the local wood. She did mad parabolas of exploration, looping further and further from the group until one of us was forced to set off in hot pursuit, shouting her name and waving dog treats wildly in the air to entice her back. It seemed to be her mission here, as everywhere else she went outdoors, to fill the entire space, to cover the territory and tame it with her tracks. The problem in this place was obvious: one small dog in a vast and ungovernable terrain. North Yorkshire has always laughed in the face of would-be conquerors, and it certainly laughed at Muffin that day. She quickly exhausted herself with her efforts, fast and furious and futile as they were. It was too rough, and too cold, even to stand and sniff, so the familiar tools in her repertoire – smell, piddle, round up and flatten – came to nothing.

She looked like a little banshee lost in a hurricane when we finally fastened her at the collar and beat a grateful retreat to the local pub. Unusually for the region, no dogs were allowed inside, so Muffin was attached to the somewhat Dickensian ring of iron by the front door. Every so often I would dart outside and feed her handfuls of doggy choc drops, but she was not appeased. Soon she started to whine, and then to howl, for all the world like a canine Cathy calling for Heathcliff up on the 'wily, windy moor'.

When we took her home, she slept for hours. Her first trip into the big outdoors had been somewhat fraught, and had left her ragged round the edges for sure, but she loved it nonetheless. Never did she turn down the offer of a walk after that, all through her long life, until she was simply too sick and old to manage. It wasn't long before the moors and the woods of her native county became her lifeblood, the body of her existence and her greatest, enduring pleasure.

Today it is cold and wet outside. It's early April 2012, and the promising heatwave of March has long subsided into a miserable drizzle of a season. This morning I lay down next to my dog for a long, long time. This is the habit we acquired years ago, doing what I euphemistically call my 'exercises', which in reality means lying very still on my back, with my knees up, vaguely incorporating the principles of the Alexander technique, but mainly gazing blankly at the ceiling whilst the dog snoozes at my side. Lately, this little ritual has fallen out of fashion in the house. Muffin's habits have changed, and so, I suppose, have mine. But we were back in the old routine today and it was very soothing. After a while, I turned on my side and watched the dog dreaming.

Muffin often sleeps with her eyes open these days, an unnerving practice in its mimicry of catatonia, even death, but it has its uses. Now that she is blind, it might not change her awareness much if the eyes are open or closed. There seems to be something else going on, however. Muffin was always alert to noise and change. She could switch from deep unconsciousness to full flight-or-fight mode in a split second. That still goes on, in muted form, though the stimulus that makes her suddenly lift her head or stumble to her feet seems entirely internal these days – a response to memory or instinct rather than external reality. Having her eyes open seems connected to this process. If she closes them for too long, maybe they will never open again, and maybe the dog, at some deep and primitive level, knows that? In any case, it seems to me that Muffin, lying there like an old crumpled handkerchief on the floor beside me, eyes occasionally drooping but mainly open, gazing at something far away and hopefully beautiful, is not quite ready to go yet, not prepared to sew her eyes together in perpetual sleep. And even though she is hard to handle these days, with her physical woes and her geriatric eccentricity, that knowledge makes me glad.

The first time Muffin nearly drowned was in Gledhow Valley Woods. This was in January 2000. I wanted to take a long walk with her, so we wandered up the hill opposite our house and took a left turn through the old gateway into an expansive piece of woodland that was once part of a monastic estate, later connected to Gledhow Hall and owned by the great and the good of Leeds, but now just another block of private flats. These woods are spectacularly steep. A thick settlement of trees lines either side of a glacial valley, with Gledhow Valley Road snaking through the centre of it, and Gledhow Lake, a low-lying expanse of water, nestling at one side of the road. The whole area is a

designated nature area and important geological site, and boasts
an unusual and prolific colony of wild birds. It is starkly beautiful in the winter, lush and abundant in summer. It is hard to
remember, when you are walking through, that this is the middle
of a city, with large housing estates, shopping centres, schools,
a hospital, a hospice and several churches, plus a Jewish temple,
all within a stone's throw. The road that drops down to the central artery, along the outer rim of the woods, encloses an area
called Little Switzerland, and it is easy to see why. Something
about the height, the sharp overhang, the sudden sloping curves
of the road and the ever-constant umbrella of trees feels very
European and ancient.

Every piece of land that is populated by trees feels special,
unique. There is a hush and a rootedness: layer upon layer of
leaves and the husks of fruit – the product of countless seasons
as they ebb and flow – all trodden down into the rich fertile earth
beneath. Each wood is different, its character colourful and distinct. Gipton Wood, our local stamping ground, has a buzzing
and friendly air. It is a much-used thoroughfare for dog walkers, schoolchildren and shoppers. Gledhow Valley Woods has a
much loftier, more regal atmosphere. There is something remote
in its aspect, austere. I never feel quite safe there, which is both
unnerving and invigorating. Muffin's character, too, used to
change when we went to Gledhow. Gipton Wood was like her
canine nursery school, full of dog pals and people and friendly
familiarity. In Gledhow Valley Woods, she ran a little wilder. It
called to her more feral nature, particularly in the early days.

This January morning she surpassed herself – and nearly wrote her own obituary at the tender age of three. The landscape was bare and bony, and it was a typically grey winter's day. There was no one else about and Muffin was wildly cheerful, scuttling here and there, scaring squirrels and breaking birds' cover with a fantastic squawk from them and a cacophony of barking from her. The first part of the walk was straightforward enough, along a narrow, sturdy pathway, which was high but even. But as we got further into the wood, looping round and down with the path, the territory changed from a steady plain to a sharp descent. We would have been all right if we had obediently stuck to the established path, which took the walker gently downwards by a series of turns and curves, but neither Muffin nor I ever had much truck with good behaviour. If there was a choice between a well-kept tidy route and an unkempt tangle off to the side, we usually chose the chaos. Thus, on this particular morning, we found ourselves suddenly on the steepest slope of the valley – nothing but bare earth held in place by the gnarled and ancient roots of trees. The dog went crazy, circling me in a giddy gallop from low to high and back again, as if she were on the switchback at a fair and loving every second.

Rather too late, I noticed the lake at the bottom of the slope. There was an odd man-made construction of steep-sided brickwork containing this part of the water – nearly impossible to get out of, once inside, particularly if you were a rather small dog – but all this was hidden from view by a kind of high informal platform reaching out over the lake. On the ridge were four smug ducks sitting in a row. Suddenly, Muffin saw the ducks and gave chase. What she did not know – and neither did I – was that beyond the ridge was a sheer drop into deep, dank water. She gave spectacular flight, scattered the ducks and plummeted, like a cartoon hound, straight down into the depths below. When I got to the edge, I saw her way beneath me, paddling frantically to keep herself afloat. It is the most I have ever seen this landlubber of a dog swim, and she definitely saved her own life by doing so with such vigour. I had no chance of reaching her, so I just ran lower down to the water's edge, shouting her name over and over to encourage her out. To this day I have no idea how she managed it, but she found the shallowest exit and staggered halfway up the steep bricks, and I pulled her out the rest of the way. It seems that there is some kind of problem with drainage and pollution in this stretch of water. As a result, the dog stank to high heaven, and was filthy black and soaking wet. We had to walk a mile home. It was a hot soapy bath for her and a double brandy for me, then we slept it off.

Of all her baptisms down the years, in sea, river and lake, this was by far the most dramatic and terrifying. Her escape was a vivid demonstration of this dog's utter determination to *live* and a sign of the courage she has consistently shown in pursuing what has been a life to admire. Her own long brilliant day in the sun.

*

Ours is a family where books and screens prevail: Tim was an avid watcher of films; I read all the time. Even before I could decipher the letters, at barely eighteen months old, I would sit on a blanket in the back garden, still as a stone and grave as the Buddha, turning the pages of a slim Victorian volume called *Progress and Poverty*. My daughter, like her dad, is a visual person – absorbing dark film thrillers deep into the night, and peppering her time with occasional reading marathons. Muffin, in this regard, was, from the very beginning, the Great Interrupter. Print and image meant nothing to her. I know some dogs who can decipher the television screen, breaking into barks of fury whenever a dog appears, but Muffin just ignored the whole thing. Her version of a good read, or a favourite film, was simply to be outdoors. Should she catch a whiff of a new scent on the breeze, when the back door was open, she would lift her head and pause, 'reading' the information with all the complicated intelligence that lay inside her twitching nostrils. Her nose contained multitudes. Her legs covered miles in pursuit of the smells revealed.

Like Molly as a small child, Muffin regarded the natural world as one huge playground just for her. She turned me into a nature lover after long adult years spent in big cities, indoors, poring over my books. She took me to places I would never dare go alone: onto isolated hillsides, into the woods and along lonely rivers. When Tim was alive, he was the solitary explorer, marching off with the dog on his own adventures. When Molly was young, the dog was a family playmate, the walks short and local, and primarily about throwing a ball, chasing a child's trike, scootering, skipping and playing hide-and-seek. In later years, when puberty claimed my daughter and Tim was gone, the dog and I were left as constant and joyful walking companions. Now every step of those jaunts together is imprinted on my mind. Twice, sometimes three times a day, we roamed outside. Even when the territory was parochial and familiar, the repetition itself felt powerful and refreshing.

Walking with a dog gives you a new perspective. When I am alone, my stride is linear, the focus forward, the feet intent on arrival. With Muffin, my attention sprawled happily. On our twice-daily visits to Gipton Wood, we were permanently distracted by other dogs, their owners, and the constant delicate changes in the surrounding flora and fauna as the seasons waxed and waned. These subtleties are undetectable in unfamiliar territory. This fine-tuned awareness is the joy of the well-trodden path. (Strange land is a different kind of thrill.)

Spring was always the prize in Gipton Wood. Like much of the North Leeds woodland, which spreads across the top of the city in a broad, beneficent green swathe, wild bluebells pack the undergrowth when the weather turns to warm. Come late April and early May, the ground of our little wood was always covered in the heavenly blue of thousands, maybe millions, of bluebells, more and more coming each year, in an ever-ripening magic carpet. A brilliant sky dropped to earth. Tim loved the bluebells and walked amongst them for hours. Muffin seemed to love them too. She took particular delight in romping through the thickest

displays, pausing to baptise a fair few with her trail-setting pid-
dles, before tearing off again into the blue. She looked
particularly fetching then, her black shiny coat against the soft
blue haze of flowers and the lush dark green of their sturdy supporting stems.

Controversy rages about the recent invasion of the more
thuggish Spanish bluebell, and these have definitely colonised
the wood alongside the natives. The Spanish flower is fatter,
paler blue, with an upright habit. The indigenous variety is altogether a more exquisite creature, its smaller head hanging coyly
to one side, the richness of its colour almost indigo in places, its
essence quite magical and ethereal. But I am from solid mongrel
stock and so is my dog. Neither of us minded the mixing of the
bloods too much. We just rejoiced at the annual festival of
flowers.

By mid-June every year, those flowers are long gone,
replaced with a forest of bracken, fern and bramble underfoot
and a feast of green overhead. The wood was originally an oak
wood, giving its name to Oakwood, the area surrounding it.
Now it is primarily beech, with some horse chestnut, sycamore
and hornbeam, and the occasional stalwart old oak. Muffin identified the wood in a totally different manner: through the
keenness of her nose, the delicate discernment of light and shade
in front of her eyes, the feel of the paths and diversions beneath
her paws.

Summer was brilliant for the dog in one respect: she could
disappear completely. She has never been an entirely obedient

hound, trotting demurely at my heels. If I stop still, she will wait for me, but if I am in motion, then so is she. Her walks, especially in her youth, were always her wild time. I never cured her of pulling breathlessly on her lead as she made her impatient way forward to that critical, anticipated moment when she was unclipped from the collar – and was free. Once off the lead, she was away with the wind, describing her wonderful spirals of movement, ears flying, tail aloft, like a little canine Ariel in Shakespeare's *Tempest*, telling master Prospero, 'I drink the air before me, and return/ Or ere your pulse twice beat.'

I never worried – not in the early days at least – because her hearing was sharp and pure, and the training I had done with her as a new dog had taken firm root in her brain. A couple of high-pitched calls of her name and she would be back, panting, laughing, happy. Nothing seemed to stand in her way when she was off on one of her adventures. She would rip through brambles, her exceptionally thick fur protecting her from injury, and she would set sail over fallen tree trunks with a seemingly effortless grace.

Other dogs were all friends to her, and she soon knew the regulars in the wood, treating them with different categories of behaviour – flirtatious, playful, respectful or motherly – depending on size, age and attractiveness. (She had very good taste in men and her two biggest crushes – Caspar and Snoop – were indeed handsome, dashing devils. Mr Darcy was definitely her style.) The trouble came only if she were on the lead and we encountered a dog bigger than her running free. Panic made her aggressive, which led her into unwise confrontations, and I had to lift her up out of harm's way on several occasions. Something in Muffin could never be tamed. She was always tilting at windmills, and I loved her for it.

Autumn and winter were wistful seasons for our walks. The multicoloured carpet of leaves in our wood, come October and November, was fun to wade through, and Muffin invariably ended up wearing a leaf or two in her hair, just like a 'thin gipsy thief', to steal a Leonard Cohen phrase. Winter was always stark. The species were, with the exception of some shiny holly trees, all deciduous, so it was like walking through a tree graveyard, the bones of their feet poking out from the earth, their skeleton arms outstretched, wide and black, to the sky, as if they had been buried where they stood and were now desperately pushing upwards to escape.

The snow, when it came, filled the little dog with delight. She found the whole thing hilarious – jumping up to her armpits in the shallow drifts and snuffling and snorting through the gathering piles of slush at the sides of the paths. The thick snow falling onto her dark coat looked beautiful, with the design of the snowflakes etched onto her black background, but the smell of wet dog upon our return, with the damp steaming from her fur and giving off a stale, intensely musky odour, was not the most pleasant of household aromas.

There are unusual birds in Gipton Wood – lesser spotted something or others – as occasional visits from earnest twitchers with cameras and binoculars prove – but the bird companions we found were ordinary enough, and no less beloved for that. Blackbirds, my favourite, would run for cover across the woodland floor, with their curious, flat-footed gait. And there were two resident robins by the north gate, bold as brass, who would follow us from bush to bush in search of treats. An elderly man, who walked there with his spaniel, used to feed them; I never did, but they didn't give up hope or harassment. At ground level, there were always squirrels, flushed from their resting or burying places by a furious Muffin, who chased them endlessly up trees, barking her head off in dismay as they disappeared yet again to the highest branches. We never saw hedgehogs, as they were far too shy and cautious, but there was much evidence of burrowing bees in the summer, a waft of butterflies and the distant sound of the woodpecker, ever present but always out of sight.

I am describing a very ordinary scene here: just a woman and her dog delighting in the everyday sights and sounds of an ancient little English wood. These commonplaces are the things to treasure, when memory has to replace experience, and when the daily dog walk becomes no longer a chore but a wistfully recalled comfort and delight, slowly receding into history.

Until she was very old and blind, Muffin was a keen and reliable gardening companion. She remained meticulous about using only the designated grass and pathways – never intruding on the flowers unless a wayward tennis ball found its way, irresistibly, into the deepest foliage. I loved having her with me while I worked and weeded, whether in my garden at home or on the wilder plot of land up at the allotment. There was such easy and obvious enjoyment in her presence: lying contentedly on her side in the summer sun; bursting into the occasional paroxysm of ecstatic rolling, her back legs akimbo, her whole torso wriggling in a ridiculous, happy fanfare.

Though she was always with me on my rougher walks, in woods and by water, she never did visits of official gardens. Mostly, dogs were forbidden anyway, but there was one honourable exception: Parcevall Hall. As its name suggests, this is a fine and elegant place, out in the dramatic hills and valleys of Wharfedale, North Yorkshire, and it is quite exceptional in its tranquillity and secret beauty. Bought as an abandoned farmhouse on a bare, bleak hillside in 1927 by romantic visionary Sir William Milner, Parcevall was transformed into a beautiful, tree-lined estate, now part of English Heritage – the building a religious retreat, its grounds open to any discerning visitor. There is a photograph of Sir William in the back of the guidebook, his face offering a shy smile, his left arm wrapped lovingly around a large golden Labrador, whose demeanour is every bit as patrician as his owner's, and who clearly adored and protected his master. The picture is appropriate.

Every part of this estate suggests the presence of the spirit – whether in animal, plant or celestial form. The highest point of the garden, the cliff walk, is 270 metres above sea level. Trollers Gill, the steep angular valley below, is said to be haunted. On dark and turbulent nights – or so goes the myth – the howling of a huge spectral hound, the Barghest, resounds against the ancient rock face, aiming to terrify the innocent passer-by. Shades of this world and the next lurk in every corner here. The whole place is like a beautiful, mournful beast, lying draped over the moody Yorkshire landscape.

The first time I visited Parcevall, the sun was shining; it was high summer. Every time I have been since, it has rained. The wet and the cold do not diminish its astonishing beauty, however – from the bamboo thickets of Tarn Ghyll Wood below, through the vivid red-flowering borders of the formal terraces, to the delicacy of the limestone rock garden right at the top.

This was never a place to let the dog off the lead. When she was with me, she was quiet and muted, adjusting her mood to the towering mystery of the landscape around her. In some environments, Muffin could look dominant and imposing. Gipton Wood was her personal fiefdom, and there she was queen. At Parcevall Hall, among the unforgiving heights and plummets of the Yorkshire Dales, she seemed tiny, like a little black hairy insect lost inside a giant flower. She caught my mood, as ever, on these Parcevall visits, because I often went there when I felt lonely and brooding. The majesty of the place reflected such reveries and deepened them; it didn't judge or jolly me out of them, the way a more gaudy garden might. In the same way, the dog was a sympathetic shadow, weaving her delicate way beside me, perfectly happy to be sad, if that were what the occasion demanded.

*

Solitary walks were a favourite and consoling daily pastime for
me in the years after my husband had died and my daughter
had crossed into the secret world of adolescence – solitary, but
never lonely. I may not have had a human companion by my
side, but I always had my dog, until Muffin's descent into ill
health and extreme old age, has stopped her from accompanying me. There is nothing to stop me walking on my own, except
a deep, nonsensical feeling that I am betraying the dog somehow by going without her. I realise that every inch of the
wonderful wood and parkland that surrounds us locally, and
the huge expanse of dale and moorland in the outlying countryside, is embedded in my mind with the memory of my dog.
It will be a strange endeavour to rediscover these places, as
inevitably I must, without the little beast beside me. Already I
am ringing friends with dogs to see if I can go with them when
they walk, so firmly linked for me are the words WALK and
DOG.

Gipton Wood is barely a hundred metres down the road from
the house. Muffin and I have not been there for four months,
since the turn of the year, when her mobility started to be compromised by the semi-collapse of her lower spine. I keep telling
myself to go on my own. It is bluebell season. The wood will be
at its finest. But something stops me every time. These days the
association of woods and water is inevitably elegiac. Layers and
layers of memory lie scattered on the woodland floor, like rich,
rotting humus, or one of those very old, twisted pieces of dead
wood, split from the growing tree and cast to one side, hollowed

out, abandoned, yet part of the fabric of the landscape itself, essential to it.

When I first got Muffin, I had notions of training her to suit our needs as a family. Little did I know how much she would train *us* about the very essence of life itself. A dog teaches you to look with different eyes, to see things from ground level, to notice little quirky details in the natural world around you, to focus on the flow of life away from all forbidding notions of timetables or clocks. Though I'm naturally an indolent person, well imbued with the work ethic nonetheless, Muffin always helped me to 'waste time' generously. She made me more childlike and wondering – never more so than on our ritualistic walks, tramping here, there and everywhere, but always, most essentially, coming back to the centre of things, back to our happy selves.

Chapter Six

Transitions

Back in 1999, at Muffin's very first check-up, when the vet detected a heart murmur and said, 'We'll have to keep an eye on this,' we just nodded sagely and took her away. From then on, life bowled along without incident, but we knew the score. This dog ran on adrenalin, and her heart beat as fast as an African drum from the very start. The vet's concern was the irregularity, as well as the speed, of her cardiac rhythms. At a symbolic level, this was poignant in itself: we had a dog whose heart simply worked too hard, too fast.

For the next ten years, Muffin sailed (sometimes literally) through her life. Nothing stopped her – except a closed door. That she always hated, especially one closed in her face, which brought an almost immediate howl of protest. The dog wanted to run, and she wanted to be beside us at all times. If those two elements were present in her life, then she was happy. She was, indeed, a very contented dog. She spent her days, when not sprawled out on the carpet snoring, watching out for us. There was never a waking moment when she was not tracking our progress, from the first bleary footsteps on the stair to make an early morning cup of tea to the drawing of the curtains and the final locking of the back door – the signal that she could now go to bed, because her long shift was over.

Muffin has always been an enormously affectionate dog. Until age and indifference quietly crept in, we could rely on her absolutely to bolster our spirits and knock the edges off any sour mood or bad temper. The minute we returned from any excursion without her, she would come running and jumping with delight to welcome us home. If I opened the back door wide enough, she would dash out into the garden and complete several laps of honour at breakneck speed, running so fast she would often fall over in her mad excitement, only to bounce right back up again, gasping for more.

She adored her family, elevating the term 'unconditional love' into a whole new category – transcendent, sublime. This was particularly gratifying for me as a single parent, since I had to weather the choppy years of my daughter's adolescence without support or respite. At least I always knew that the dog loved me without restraint. In fact, it was a love that could be cloying. If Muffin were in a room with me and I got up, then inevitably she would jump up too. If I left the room, she would follow, close on my heels. Never officially allowed upstairs, except for meditation sessions and, latterly, for afternoon naps, whenever she did climb the steps with me, it was essential to hold onto the banister, otherwise she would trip me up, so close was she weaving behind.

Her gaze was penetrating and alert. The fight-or-flight mechanism, honed in the pack during her first three turbulent years before rescue, was never switched off. Even when fast asleep, the slightest noise could rouse her: a knock at the door would send her into a paroxysm of defensive barking. She took her duties very seriously indeed. She seemed indomitable, immortal, but things caught up with her in the end.

By 2009, Muffin had been with us for a full decade and was coming up to thirteen years old. She was suddenly middle aged – elderly in dog years – and the cracks were beginning to show. A strange symptom started up during the summer of 2009: whenever we arrived home and the dog leapt up to greet us, she would be overcome by a choking and coughing fit – one she seemed to resolve only by a sort of vomiting action to release the airways in her throat and calm her system down. Muffin's vet was puzzled and, without seeing the fit in progress, he could not definitively diagnose the cause, but he had a feeling it was her soft palate, grown flabby with age, causing an obstruction on sudden movement or excitation.

Whatever it was, it caused alarm. The noises the dog made to regain her equilibrium were loud and distressing. It made the whole business of homecoming less a joyous celebration, as before, and more a surreptitious worry. What could we do to get in quietly and stop the dog fussing? Muffin was a naturally loving and demonstrative dog. It was impossible. It was like telling her not to care. She just couldn't do it. The outbursts seemed to be worse when I came in, since I was designated

Leader of the Pack in Tim's absence, so I took to sneaking in behind Molly, as if I had never been away, taking the house by stealth. Muffin was rarely fooled: she was up and choking before I knew it. We coped. She coped. She was a tough little creature. The second the coughing fit was finished, it was as if it had never happened, and she carried on with her life regardless. The tick tock of the clock, however, was inexorable. Time seemed less of a generously given thing now, careless in its abundance, but borrowed, subtly precarious. Finite.

In the autumn of 2009, I paid a visit to Hungary, a country I had lived and worked in twenty years previously, and which laid claim to a large (somewhat neglected) part of my heart. There was the usual kerfuffle over domestic arrangements. Molly was easy – she stayed with friends – but I always wrestled with the dog conundrum. There were the helpful cousins and some dog-loving friends who helped out whenever they could, but it is a big ask, foisting your animal onto someone else. Nobody ever complained, and Muffin was usually a polite and amenable house guest. Still, there was always a nagging doubt at the back of my mind.

Muffin came to us as a dog with a bundle of neuroses. It quickly became clear that the penalty for her rapid attachment to us as her new owners was an acute separation anxiety, which manifested particularly in a closed-door syndrome. Taking her to dog kennels was out of the question, as this was too similar to being in the rescue pound, a place she had hated and feared with a venom, howling the place down, day and night. It was a year or two, also, before we dared leave her with anyone else, and then it was with Tim's cousins, who were supremely confident and skilful dog handlers. We struck lucky there.

Back in the early days, there had been a desperate incident once when we left her in the house of some friends, with suitcases packed in the hall for a later departure, only to come back to ripped carpets and smashed bowls, Muffin having gone into a frenzy of destructiveness at the very thought that we might not return; the suitcases were the trigger. The flat she wrecked was immaculate. My blood still turns to ice at the very memory. After that, I was cautious, to the point of lunacy, whenever she was in the care of someone else.

Muffin was oblivious to all this: she was a total princess. She loved being pampered and petted. The more attention lavished on her, the more she sparkled and shone. At home it was plain food and simple surroundings, but this particular autumn, in 2009, she went to stay in a huge and beautiful house with two Leeds friends, Catherine and Joe. They spoiled her rotten. The strict food rules were thrown out of the window. Catherine cooked up special batches of chicken. Joe used his 'animal whisperer' skills to charm the dog into easy submission. They took her on massive walks round the park, with slap-up meals to follow. To top it all, she went out one day with a crowd of strapping rugby players, sitting on their knees in the back of the car on the way home like the flirty little good-time girl she was. Returning home after this particular holiday was a bit of a comedown for her. Afterwards, any hint of staying at the Big House always brought a bright-eyed and happy response, from the minute she got out of the car to trot up the lavender-lined path to the front door, to the crossing of the threshold for an invariably warm, loving welcome. She treated the place as if it were her own, as she learned to do with all the special homes that she stayed in. As the years went by, she came to expect strokes and attention, rather than the neglect and abuse of her early years, as her absolute right in life. Justice, in this regard, was duly served.

Hungary was never a place I associated with dogs. When I had worked there in the theatre in 1989, it was as much as the actors could do to look after themselves, let alone a child or animal. The East Europeans are enthusiastic drinkers and decidedly chaotic in their personal lives – at least, the artists I knew among them were. But during the years I was away, everything had changed: the regime, the culture, the people themselves. Relationships were formed; children were born. A sense of domestic stability had crept in, as if by stealth, or perhaps it was just the natural process of growing up and ageing.

Anyway, on my first visit back after two decades, several dogs trotted across my path and into my conversations. It was on this trip that my friend István described at length how the gift of a small dog had saved his mother from despair – taking her out of the flat where she lived alone, into the hills of old Buda, to wander about with her canine companion, striking up conversations with all sorts of people she would normally ignore. A dog is such a great leveller, whether in the woods of northern

England or on the beautiful rolling riverbanks of old Europe – dog behaviour and dog language are universal.

One day I spotted an actor acquaintance – someone I dimly remember hanging off billiard tables into the wee hours of the morning in the theatre green room, with a cigarette drooping from one hand, a large glass of wine permanently affixed to the other – rather demurely exercising his happy black dog around the theatre grounds, not a fag nor a wine bottle anywhere in sight. I had never seen this man in broad daylight before! Sometimes a dog can help you clean up your act, and your mind, when nothing else can.

The dog that really moved me on this visit was the street urchin rescued by the daughter of a costume and set designer friend in Kaposvár. Kaposvár is a bonny country town in the south-west of Hungary, which boasts a major repertory theatre and was one of the places where I had worked in the late 1980s. Stefi, the daughter, is a meltingly pretty girl, with long, dark hair and shining eyes. The delicacy of her looks matches the tenderness of her heart. She has a long track record of rescuing waifs and strays. This particular autumn it was a small, painfully thin dog, white haired and mottled with black, that had been found roaming the streets, abandoned. Stefi had brought the dog home, tenderly feeding it tasty morsels, and slowly, painstakingly, building up trust between her and the freaked-out little animal. The dog was terrified of people – and had probably incurred more than her fair share of kickings and abuse – so Stefi kept her quiet and safe, taking her for walks at night, when there were fewer pedestrians around and much less traffic, and generally acting as her devoted guardian angel.

I asked if I could see the dog, which Stefi kept in her room when visitors came. She was reluctant, but then agreed, carrying her out like a baby, slowly, protectively. I extended the back of my hand towards the dog's nose for her inspection. Despite the quietness and friendliness of the move, she instantly recoiled. I kept my distance after that, and Stefi soon put her back in her room, as if she were a rescued hostage, only slowly being acclimatised to the outside world. I was struck, as I saw the two together, girl and dog, by how similar they seemed. Each was disarmingly beautiful, shimmering with a painful, palpable vulnerability.

The dogs we are attracted to, and who are attracted to us, reflect so much of our inner nature. The actor in the park was a sturdy fellow, not much given to introspection or reflection. His dog, rootling around happily in the bushes, was of a similar ilk. They were pals, the relationship functional and fun. Stefi, blooming, in late adolescence, like a fresh spring flower, had found in her rescue dog a quite different kindred spirit. It seemed, watching them, as if they were two naked hearts, beating together: an invisible delicate thread joining them indelibly, one to the other. My relationship with Muffin was never that rarified, but the invisible thread – extendable, pliant, yet strong – was always in place.

When I got back from Hungary, I was particularly keen to see Muffin. There was always the lurking fear that she would have supplanted me in her affections whilst I was away, but this has never happened. When I rang the doorbell at my friend's house, there was a familiar cacophony of barking, followed by a squirming mass of black fur, as she wriggled impatiently through the newly opened door. Always, after a period away from her, I had to adjust my memory. She was much smaller, shaggier and more intensely black than I remembered. One thing was consistent: her love was undiminished – if not deepened – after every separation. It never failed to make my own heart lift.

Christmas 2009 was special, although we did not know it at the time. It was to be the last Christmas we spent with my father, who died early the following year. Dad had spent several festive seasons with Molly, Muffin and me in Leeds, and he was always a hilarious, if somewhat demanding house guest. My dad was a natural-born lotus-eater. One of the first memories a former colleague had of him as a young, newly qualified lecturer was of Dad waving a champagne bottle around at some gathering and begging people to fill up their glasses. He relished his food and worshipped Bacchus above all other gods. A meal out was never complete for him without three, often four, different glasses around his plate: one for lager, one for wine, a small one for water and possibly another one for a different colour wine. The trick of keeping him happy in his dotage was to turn the heating up, keep the television on for the afternoon quiz shows, provide a daily paper for the crossword, keep him topped up

with food and drink every few hours and give him the best bedroom in the house, with permission to sleep as long and as often
as he wanted. If those needs were met, he was charm itself: witty,
naughty, subversive.

He loved dogs and was very tender towards all creatures. He
recognised their sensitivities and respected them. Muffin, in her
turn, loved him. They often sat and watched television together,
the dog benefiting from the 'crumbs' that dropped from Dad's
plate with alarming regularity. Since Muffin's digestion had
always been poor – she has never fully recovered from her early
starvation diet – the pair of them had to be watched closely, otherwise accidents would ensue. The larger the 'accidental' piece
of ham that found its way from the man's plate to the dog's jaws,
the more likely it was that I, as chief mopper-up of all messes,
would suffer the consequences the next morning, when Muffin
failed to hold it all in until she got outside.

The fathers in the extended family were particularly prone
to dog spoiling; the mothers had more sense. Whenever we went
to Tim's parents for Sunday lunch, the dog would wriggle her
way immediately to the far end of the table and sit, shiny-eyed
and expectant, by my father-in-law's chair and fix him with an
unblinking, melting look of longing. He found it absolutely
impossible to resist her, and vast amounts of meat, potato and
pie would find their way from his plate to her mouth before
anyone could call a halt to proceedings and haul the dog away.
My own father was a little more restrained, but his temperament
and reasoning were essentially the same: 'The dog looks hungry:

let's feed the dog. If I feed the dog, the dog will love me.' Of course, both men were right.

Muffin liked Dad for more than the treats he gave her: she also liked his stillness. She listened when he crooned to her in silly nonsense language. She softened when he scratched her ears and stroked her long, narrow back. She had enjoyed many summer visits to my parents' house in Essex, running the length of their extensive garden and losing countless tennis balls over the fence and in the overgrown borders. She came to recognise the pattern of Christmas: when the tree was up and the lights were twinkling, then she knew that soon the old gentleman would arrive and start to feed her with crackers and paté and slivers of pork pie, like her very own Santa Claus.

Crisis never strikes cleanly. If something bad happens, it is normally twisted up with some other disaster or complication. There are years that sail past in a froth of light-heartedness, or are simply uneventful, but then there are years when every-thing that can go wrong does – dark years of challenge and hardship, lost times. 2010 was such a year for me. The winter had been tough and long. The snow came early and it lingered. By February, with the skies still leaden with sleet and snow, and the ground still frozen underfoot, people were tired and run-down.

The weather took its toll, particularly on my father, who was thin and frail at eighty-six, and found it hard to move around even in clement weather, with a seriously arthritic knee forcing him to use sticks and crutches for the shortest walk. The snow was seriously hampering his mobility and his mood.

One grey morning in February, he rang me up for a quick chat. He sounded tense and anxious: a blocked ear canal had made him even deafer than usual, and it was packed full of olive oil and cotton wool, ready to be syringed the next day. It was tormenting him and, in retrospect, may have indicated something else – a slow-brewing storm in the brain – about to hit. We didn't have much to say to each other, and the call was short, but it was the last time we ever spoke. I often think that I should have told him I loved him, but I trust he was safe in that knowledge.

The same evening, I had a call from a friend who had just received bad news from a cancer scan, and rushed round to sit with her. While I was there, I got a confused mobile phone message to say that Dad had been in a car accident and was in hospital, unconscious. No one knew much more than that, but already my heart was in my boots. Throughout six decades of driving, my father had hardly so much as scratched his car. He prided himself on his exemplary record and no claims bonus. Something had gone seriously wrong.

When I got home, my daughter rushed down the stairs to meet me, and we decided, somewhat tearfully, that I would have to travel the 200 miles to Essex the next day, whilst she – now seventeen, and very self-contained – held the fort at home. Everything about the situation seemed bleak. Meanwhile, as my daughter stood on the stairs, two steps above me, with me at the bottom, looking up, there was, as ever, a third witness in the unfolding drama – the dog. There she lay, mute and obedient, in her basket in the hall.

Highly charged scenes in real life occur like this: in doorways, on steps, in unexpected corners, never in a grand, prepared arena. Everything significant, it seems, slips sideways into – and out of – the world. When I took the call that Tim had just died, I was standing in another hallway, in our previous house. Muffin had been there too, taking it all in, absorbing the weight of the atmosphere around her, unable to cut herself off – to save herself – from the grieving people to whom she was so connected. This time, my father was not yet dead, but the scene itself felt familiar, and intuition was giving me fatal clues.

When I left for Essex, early the next morning, Muffin came with me. The hours Molly spent at school – and at her job in the art department after school – were too long for the dog to endure alone. In any case, she had been present at every significant family event; there was no reason to think that this would be different. I picked up my nephew en route. We arrived, in thick fog and snow and treacherous conditions, to find that my father had suffered a massive stroke whilst driving. The car crashed when he lost consciousness at the wheel. Thankfully, no one else was involved, but that was the only thing to be thankful for.

When we visited him at the hospital, he was utterly transformed from the jolly man I had hosted at Christmas barely two months before. Stripped of his clothes and glasses, he looked small and broken under the hospital sheets. I spoke to him, but don't know if he heard, and held his hand, but cannot say that he felt my touch. Although this was in the natural order of things – for the parent to fade before the child – it was still a massive sorrow and a shock. Within a few days, Dad was dead. He never really regained consciousness.

What happened during those weeks in February is now a bit of a blur: a chaos of journeys back and forth along the snow-packed motorways; a muddle of post-death administration; and valiant attempts by my two brothers and me to cope with the inevitable turmoil precipitated by sudden death. Muffin was con-stantly by my side. She came to the hospital and waited in the car. She went for the shortest of walks and endured the longest of time doing nothing, and being ignored, as we all tried to make sense of a grievous situation. At no point did she complain – whine, bark or pester. She simply made herself available when needed, and all but invisible when the house was too full of people for there to be much room for a small dog as well. Who knows what sense, if any, she made of it all? One thing became abundantly clear, once we were back home and life began to settle down a bit: the experience had taken its toll on the dog, as well as the humans. She had not emerged unscathed.

Everybody has a faultline – a symptom that recurs when we are under great strain in our lives, when something is being sup-pressed, or heavily borne. For me, when the going gets tough, it is backache from an old dance injury that floors me, literally, since it makes me lie flat. For my daughter, it is sickness and nausea. For Muffin, it has always been that damned cough, that treacherous heart. When we got back from Essex after my father's death, the dog was very tired and muted. She looked as if the stuffing had been knocked right out of her, and I knew just how she felt.

Although he was old and physically fragile, Dad had been a rock to lean on in the years following my husband's and then my mother's death. We clung to the wreckage together, recognising the loneliness of losing a partner in each other's eyes. Though we were more often apart than together, we both enjoyed the other's company enormously. We laughed a lot. And Dad filled the role of paterfamilias in our small, all-female household. I missed him terribly. And when I looked at Muffin, I saw the light gone, too, from her normally animated and soulful gaze.

One night I heard her wheezing in her basket and rushed downstairs to find her staggering to her feet, gasping for breath, a look of panic flooding her face. This was worse than any attack she had had before. It happened several nights running, and I took her into my bedroom to keep on eye on her, jumping up several times a night to support her and try to help her breathe.

There was a vet out of town who specialised in homeopathy. He had helped Muffin before, with her firework phobia, and I had a feeling he would be particularly sensitive in this situation. I took her in one morning, and gave a brief history, including the soft palate problem and our recent bereavement. Gently, gently he looked at my shivering dog – even the kindest of vets sent her into nervous apoplexy. He listened to her heart; he looked into her troubled eyes. 'This dog is sensitive to grief,' he said. 'Her heart is under strain. The new cough is caused by that.' Too much pressure was being put on her valiant body, and on the pump that was keeping it going. He prescribed some homeopathic remedies: one for the effects of grief and the other to support her heart directly.

Later that week, some friends came to visit. I told them about the dog and what the vet had said. One of them laughed in absolute disbelief. A dog? Grief-stricken? How absurd. But I knew this dog, and it made perfect sense to me. Muffin would not know directly that Dad was dead – how could she? But she was a dog acutely sensitive to atmospheres; she was intimately connected to my mood and behaviour, and I was clearly in a state of sorrow; and, most importantly, she had been here before, and knew, with her instinctive wisdom, exactly what was going on. She was suffering too.

Biologist John Bradshaw writes that both humans and dogs, being essentially pack animals, gain benefit from mutual emotional display, unlike wild, lone creatures, who need to hide what they are feeling in order to stay on top. He also believes that dogs only exhibit the basic prime emotions of fear, anger, anxiety and happiness. He does not think them capable of more subtle responses, such as shame, embarrassment – or grief.

With this in mind, it is hard to say whether Muffin's predicament was generated by a deeply felt internal state or whether she had simply absorbed my sadness and made it her own. Either way, the dog was in distress. Where before she had managed to shake it off with the resilience and optimism of youth, now, as age overtook her, her capacity to bounce back was wounded and impaired. After years of comforting and supporting us, this was the moment at which the tables were turned. We must shield her now, and watch her as carefully and with as much love as she had always lavished on us.

Things slowly improved, as winter turned to spring. Muffin's mood lifted and the usual routine of work for me, school for Molly and wood walks for the dog was re-established. A new, shaky sort of rhythm took us forward. Muffin still loved to run – indeed it was impossible to stop her – despite her deteriorating heart. But now it seemed as if there was something almost reck-lessly defiant in her speed, as if she *would* keep pushing herself, even if it killed her.

As the weather got warmer, she panted more frequently. When she was not out on a walk, she would lie flaked out for hours in the coolest corner she could find. She had never been a fan of hot weather – her fur was too thick and long for that – and her discomfort was more obvious now, the symptoms of it more frequent. June 2010 was a very hot month indeed. Still Muffin tried to run, but she fell several days in a row, tumbling awkwardly onto her side. Usually she got herself up right away, but on one of these occasions she dropped and fainted dead away, her limbs jerking and twitching, her lips drawn back in a ghastly rictus. When it occurred again, at home, leaving the dog lying in a pool of her own urine, only to come round in dazed confusion, completely puzzled as to what had just happened, we went back to her usual vet for advice.

He, like the homeopath, confirmed the full onset of heart

disease. 'The heart is enlarged – it is stopping blood flow to the brain when she is overactive, and so she faints. Don't try and pick her up when she has an episode; let her lie still and recover. She is doing the right thing by getting her head to the ground.' The cough, he added, was linked to the same problem – Muffin's huge, generous heart was pressing on her larynx and making her choke.

The irony of this was hard to ignore: her all-too-giving heart was killing her. More pills were prescribed to shrink the distended heart, and off we went home, with another huge dent in the bank balance and another note of doom sounding in the back of the brain. But we would do what we could to keep the dog buoyant. We weren't ready to let her go yet.

Muffin, as so often, both before and after this event, proved to have remarkable powers of recovery. We resumed our twice-daily walks, and the falls became less frequent, less dramatic, but the dog was definitely slowing down. Even she was getting the message to take care. She ran a little bit, but ambled about more and, in between, she sniffed long and hard at the undergrowth, finding interest where she never had before, as if in some kind of withdrawal therapy from the chief joy of her life, SPEED. So, no more my little spritely Puck in *A Midsummer Night's Dream*, telling his master, Oberon, 'I go, I go – look how I go – / Swifter than arrow from the Tartar's bow.' Muffin was an altogether more earthbound character now, the circle of her life slowly closing.

*

There is a much-loved Hungarian novel by Antal Szerb called *Journey by Moonlight*, in which the protagonist, Mihály, goes on a nostalgic journey in search of his lost youth and the people who inhabited it. He comes across a man he was at university with, who is now a successful academic but still lives like a scruffy, idealistic student. Mihály muses, 'Here's a man who's achieved the impossible . . . A man who's managed to stay fixed at the age that suits him. Everyone has one age that's just right for him, that's certain. There are people who remain children all their lives, and there are others who never cease to be awkward and absurd, who never find their place until suddenly they become splendidly wise old men and women: they have come to their real age.'

The same is true of dogs. My aunt's dog, Trixie, was a sweet-natured black and white dog of indeterminate breed and portly physique (mainly due to her daily intake of tea and biscuits – with a bit of cake thrown in on baking day), who always seemed middle aged to me. Similarly, there are several old greyhounds who tread their soft, spidery way through the woods near us. It is impossible to imagine them young and racing, yet they seem happy in their own skin, like retired ballerinas, still elegant, but no longer driven by the need to be the prima donna.

Muffin, for her part, has always been young at heart. She was happiest, I think, at five years old, when she had been with us for a couple of years and was settled but still youthful enough to tear like wildfire through the trees, and fortunate to have a girl at home to play with, a man well enough to take her for long walks and a woman solicitous in keeping her well-fed, warm and healthy. At five, she was certainly in her pomp.

She hasn't weathered old age with much enthusiasm, and who can blame her? There are things that she has tried to do, right up until very recently – hurdles to jump, spaces to squeeze through, races to run – quite forgetful, until her body reminds her, painfully, of the fact that those gymnastics are way behind her now. Muffin's character has always been one of reckless valour to match her soulful introspection. The curtailment of her powers, the clipping of her wings, despite her customary stoicism, has been a source of some disappointment to the dog.

Today I watched a boy play with his springer spaniel. The spaniel was catching a ball, razor sharp, focused and fast. The beauty and precision of its movement was breathtaking and I felt grateful to watch. 'You are doing this for Muffin now,' I thought, as the dog leapt and ran. It was poignant, certainly, but also in the scheme of things – the passing of a baton, a simple, generational thing. Because there will always be another ball to throw and another young dog eager to jump for her life and snatch that ball in her mouth triumphantly.

Once, when I was driving down the motorway, I saw in the carriageway in front of me a heaving, shuddering mass. It was a large hare, which had obviously been hit by a car and was not yet dead but certainly in the final agonies of dying. I have never seen such death throes before or since. An epic struggle was going on, right in front of me, between the urgent will to live and the need to let go and die, and the memory has never left me.

Muffin, thankfully, has remained relatively pain-free right into old age, despite her rapidly accumulating ailments and trials. In recent years, the arthritis in her back legs has made her stiff and achy, but, as the vet has constantly reassured me, 'She is not in distress, not in real pain.' I choose to believe him because the alternative is unbearable. Nothing makes me quake more than the sight of suffering in small children and in animals. The naked injustice of it is overwhelming.

It is fitting that I have a rescue dog, because the urge to *save* is rather entrenched in my system. I once followed a woman for ten minutes down a long Underground tunnel in London because I thought she was being harassed by a strange man, who kept putting his arm round her, even though she pushed him away. In the end I ran to catch up with her and said, breathlessly, 'Is he bothering you?' to the consternation of everyone around. 'Oh no, it's OK. He's my boyfriend,' she replied. 'But thank you.' Who knows what I would have done if she had said yes? I am not known for my attack skills, and he was a big guy.

It is not just people, not just animals: these days I cannot even squash a slug. Soon I will be sweeping the streets in front of me as I walk, like those extraordinary Jain monks, in order not to step on any tiny bug – even a single-celled entity – that happens to be underfoot. So I don't find it easy to watch my beloved dog's gradual decline. I lack the aloof competence of a good nurse, and find the whole thing disconcerting.

It was a new and particularly challenging chapter in Muffin's life that started in June 2010, with that first falling swoon in the woods. She continued to cough and faint at intervals all through the summer, dropping onto her side rather gracefully, like a medieval princess, and coming round in a blur a few minutes later, only too grateful for a helping hand to get her to her feet. It was almost as if she were practising dying in these strange, unnerving interludes. I got used to the pattern of them and sat with her as she recovered each time, watching how she willed herself back to consciousness with courage and determination. You can't keep a good dog down. Not this one, anyway.

Sometimes, in a neat reversal of those dogs who can predict their owners' epileptic fits, I was able to ward off a faint by catching hold of her by the ribs and getting her to breathe deeply, just by means of my physical support. Often I could do nothing, except damage limitation – mopping up her involuntary puddles and stroking her in reassurance as she gradually came round. In time, the vet's tablets took effect, bringing down the swelling around her heart and lessening both the frequency and severity of the attacks. When she relapsed, at the end of the year, a new drug, Vivitonin, was added to her regime to enlarge the capillaries and encourage a freer flow of blood and oxygen to the brain. This worked like a charm and for over a year since then she has remained steady, and her heart – that amazing heart – has held out.

Nonetheless, the sense of lockdown that came in the wake of my father's death, inside me and in the dog, was strange and difficult for us both. Before, when one of us was down, the other was up; as in any good partnership, the strong one stepped up – or waited – for the one left behind. It was rare, this double strike. My mood was bleak, Muffin's health compromised. Molly, at eighteen, was off doing her own thing, and quite right too. My dog and I made an increasingly odd little couple. More and more, I cast an invisible protective arm over her, worrying about her when we were out, keeping her close when we were at home. This reversal of roles has a kind of symmetry to it. It is a natural levelling.

People who do not have dogs have found it hard to comprehend. That my social life should be so dictated by one small dog seems ludicrous to them. 'Oh just leave her with someone.' 'Put her in kennels' has been a familiar refrain. But the people who know me best, and certainly the ones who have met the dog and seen something of her valiance, understand perfectly. More than ever, over the past two years, Muffin and I have been joined at the hip. Love me, love my dog – or forget it.

When Muffin was rescued, she had never been in a car before. I didn't learn to drive until 2000, so it was a series of buses and trains for the first year, which she tolerated well, but cars made her sick. She never cried or jumped about; she just vomited. The answer was simple habituation. The tough love of a friend, who owns a smallholding in the North Yorkshire countryside, and therefore has a decidedly pragmatic attitude towards all animals, also helped. When we went to stay and she took us somewhere in her car, bringing her dog and ours along too, she insisted they both went in the boot. Before, Muffin had rattled about on the back seat. The new arrangement worked like a charm. From that moment, she travelled in the car boot, with a great view out of the rear window. The confined space, and concomitant sense of safety, suited her perfectly. The carsickness disappeared completely and Muffin became a brilliant car companion, quiet and peaceful in her lair at the back, a reliable and happy traveller. If she was put in the car, she knew she was coming with us, and that was all she wanted – to be on board.

Old age changed things here, too. Her arthritic legs made it harder for her to negotiate twists and bends, sending her lurching into the tight corners of the boot, where before her natural balance kept her in the centre. I needed to have her where I could see her properly, and offer a restraining hand where necessary, at traffic lights and pedestrian crossings. This led to grumpy exchanges between us. If she travelled in the front seat, I often ended up changing gear with her nose, or extracting her front paws from my lap after an unexpected bend. If she was in the back, she occasionally plummeted from her basket head first into the footwell behind the front seat, and struggled like a stranded beetle to right herself, usually without success. It took a lot of messing about with cushions and makeshift barriers before we learned how to make it work. In the end, she took control of the entire back seat, with a selection of duvets, pillows and her basket on top – total car domination, which suited her fine.

These days I rarely go anywhere at all with Muffin in the car, so small has her world become. But, undaunted by my gloom and her fainting fits, we did make one epic journey together in the late summer of 2010. Every year my brother has a summer party and invariably we go along. Muffin, indeed, is a badge-holder as one of the most loyal attendees. Martin lives four and a half hours away in leafy Berkshire – down the M1 motorway and turn right. The dog has peed regularly on the tree-lined slope at Watford Gap service station, gateway between north and south and our usual coffee stop en route. People, like dogs, are creatures of habit and ingrained comfort routines. On this journey, I wouldn't countenance a stop anywhere else. It's tradition.

This particular year the drive was complicated by a detour in and out of London – twice – to pick up a niece. Then, after the party, Muffin and I continued our odyssey down more motor-ways, in hot and sultry weather, into the deep south-west, to the heart of Cornwall. We were invited to stay with friends at their country house. Not once, in all these peregrinations, did the dog complain. Her prowess as fellow traveller, despite her failing health, remained undimmed.

Both the dog and I are similar in one respect: we are eager adventurers, polite and enthusiastic visitors, but rather anxious hosts. With me at her side, the dog will willingly perform the niceties of social interaction when out – accept pats and strokes from all sides, and then sit peacefully at my side amidst all manner of human hubbub – but should a stranger appear at the door at home, she has made a career out of being affronted. When it is unwanted visitors, I display similar symptoms.

Since Muffin is now too deaf to bark or bother, it is hard to imagine that, back in the day she was like a little Rottweiler, with her snarls and grumblings and overzealous guardianship. Even with expected guests, Muffin could be difficult until she knew them well, growling at even the friendliest of overtures and refusing to be placated. It was embarrassing but honest. She never stopped believing that it was her job, her duty and her *right* to protect her human family, even from their own friends and neighbours, nor did she enjoy being told to shut up when the protests went on too long. Invariably, when silenced, a short peevish bark or two would follow – carefully timed – some seconds after the reprimand had made her mute. Like the other women in her household, Muffin always enjoyed having the final word. Even in someone else's house, she would assume the role of tiny sentinel, because this was a dog with an overdeveloped sense of responsibility. She took the world on her shoulders, and she kept it at bay, as best she could, but otherwise, when she was an invited guest, she behaved herself.

As my Cornwall friend put it, about our stay in her house that summer of 2010, 'Muffin really tried so hard to do the right thing.' There were two bigger dogs to whom she rightly deferred, for she was pragmatic as well as polite. Though she was never above sneaking into another dog's basket, stealing their food or howling if she was shut up with them at night – so no angel, certainly. We did have rules, she and I, which evolved early, when she came to us, and which she has kept to through-out her life. First, and most important, was this: the human has precedence over the canine. Beloved though you may be, little dog, know your place. So Muffin stayed low when she was in a crowd, and did not jump up or fuss. Even when other dogs were climbing onto people's laps, sitting on best furniture and push-ing their noses into people's faces, Muffin kept her cool – mostly. Priceless indeed were the drop-dead looks she gave these vari-ous other miscreants, in different houses, down all the years, but still she knew what we had agreed.

In fact, Muffin, despite her territorial instincts, and before she got too old to be bothered, always rather liked a party. It put her back in the pack she had run with, as a young dog squashed in a tiny flat with a mass of other puppies. At any big do in our house, her usual defensiveness soon broke down. She knew she was outnumbered, so she soon stopped barking at arrivals and just milled about in the thick of it, happy to be mauled by marauding children, or fed surreptitious titbits by guests who pretended not to know our other rule – no scavenging or begging!

She particularly relished my brother's parties, because his garden is huge, and the whole event very free range, so she could lose herself whenever she felt like it and wander off for a snooze, or steal a few barbecue treats out of the black bin liners, when no one was looking. But in the past couple of years, even these simple delights have palled for her. Deafness and encroaching blindness have dulled her senses towards others. At my brother's most recent party, she hardly recognised even well-loved people, and was confused and overwhelmed by the numbers.

At a recent gathering at my house, where once she would have relished being surrounded by an animated group of visitors, lapping up the noise, the laughter and the attention, this time she hardly noticed people arrive and barely lifted her head when they left. She just dozed through the whole thing, immobile. People who knew her well were saddened and upset. Up till then Muffin had been a permanent member of the gang, but now there was no avoiding the fact the dog's party days were over.

After the summer and the long journey south – and then back north again – were successfully weathered, we slid gently into autumn. I took Molly to Paris for a weekend in October to celebrate her eighteenth birthday – another milestone, another stage of change and unpredictability. Why does life never stand still? Just one minute of suspended animation would be helpful: Muffin frozen mid-air, mid-catch; my daughter still a child, when all seemed fresh and easy, and me just turned forty, and thinking *that* was old!

Obviously, the dog did not come with us on this particular trip, although the idea of her setting off on Eurostar and trotting through the narrow bohemian streets of the Latin Quarter is a charming one. She has a certain Gallic raffishness, and would not be entirely out of place under a barstool in a little corner café. Even her toilet habits, grown unpredictable with age, would not bother the Parisians, to whom any notion of clearing up after their dogs is laughable to the point of absurd. I have spent many

a happy hour dodging piles of French dog poo on the most elegant of Right Bank boulevards. But no, Muffin stayed on English
shores, in one of the several holiday homes she accumulated
through the years: this time, with my cousins Phil and Libby in
Hertfordshire. Each partner is an enthusiastic walker, so Muffin
had gone on many a long ramble with them in the past. On this
occasion, they did not get further than their own local wood. 'I
have a feeling this might be her last visit,' mused Phil, so we took
a photograph of the three of them as a keepsake. Everyone is
disappointed that Muffin has got old. Maybe she reminds us all
rather too vividly, in her seemingly rapid decline, of just how
quickly our own lives are passing before our very eyes.

Autumn turned to winter, birthday to Christmas. There was
no amenable old Dad to share his pork pie with Muffin this year.
Did she miss him? Did she know? Who can say, but I certainly
did. There have been so many gaps this dog has bridged, so
much warm-hearted space she fills, in the name of duty and of
love.

We wrapped her presents on Christmas Eve 2010 – two soft
toys of the sort she now barely looked at, let alone played with –
and wondered if her normal delight on Christmas morning, all
those boxes, all that paper to rip, would have fizzled to nothing,
but not a bit of it. In she dived amongst all the festive fripperies,
and held each gift between her paws, delicately biting at the
paper and then spitting the bits to one side to reveal the treasure
underneath. Like small children everywhere, Muffin's chief joy
was always in the packaging and its destruction. She did not

much care what was inside. But – unlike many of those same small offspring – she tackled her Christmas lunch with unswerving enthusiasm. She would even have relished a Brussels sprout had I been foolish enough to put it in her bowl. She did get plenty of rich gravy spiked with red wine though. On Christmas Day normal food rules definitely do not apply.

There are some benefits to decrepitude. The fireworks every Guy Fawkes' Night, and on New Year's Eve – from that inauspicious beginning in December 1999, when Muffin first came to us, on the brink of the millennium – invariably sent her crazy with fear. The symptoms grew worse, year on year. She felt the noises like gunshots to the body, causing her ears and her whole nervous system real shock and pain. No amount of aversion therapy or tranquillisers ever seemed to work, although alternative therapies had some limited success. Once at my brother's house, when midnight struck and the noise began, the dog shook so hard I thought she would literally fall into pieces. We had to stay away after that. But deafness brought great relief. I was used to staying at home on 31 December, not being a fan of end-of-year excess, and aware that the dog needed attending to. But New Year's Eve 2010 passed off without a hiccup for the first time ever. Muffin barely lifted an eyebrow at the midnight mayhem – a real indication that her hearing was seriously impaired.

This was just the first of the many symptoms that started to appear, thick and fast, during her fifteenth year – all confirming my dog's entry into the very last stages of her long and brilliant career. In fact, she has rivalled Rasputin in her ability to fight off a seemingly endless stream of attempts down the years, by Mother Nature and her own reckless disposition, to kill her off. Like the mad Russian monk, she has kept coming back, and lurching boldly forward.

By the autumn of 2011, where this story began, she had already survived a heroic catalogue of ailments and accidents, culminating, in a weird mirror-image of my own father, with her midsummer stroke. All bets were off for her survival thereafter. But, for a little slip of a dog, she has a ferocious will. And, in the wake of her brain's mini collapse, the best of her determination was yet to come. I have watched her fall down over and over, both metaphorically and literally, since that unpleasant day, when some kind of bang went off in her head and sent her keeling over, in confusion and alarm.

Summer 2011 leeched into autumn, winter into spring 2012, and she has prevailed. Although seriously impaired in health, mobility and spirits, she still seems, right at the end of her life, to have some deep sense of sanctity, of veiled joy beneath the pall of her infirmity.

I have always loved this dog. She has cheered me up no end of times with her bright sense of humour, her antics often making me roar with laughter. She has kept me fit, making me walk when I only wanted to drift. She has demanded a routine, when I could easily have got lost and distracted in the dribble of daily life. She kept me going, as she has kept going herself, leading by lovely example.

All of these things are gifts, but what she is teaching me now is the most powerful and poignant thing of all. She is slipping quietly away from the world with not a hint of panic or fear. There is such dignity in her clumsy body, her awkward bones. Does she know that she, too, will die, like the people she watched die before? Of course not. She has no cognition, none of the prescience that is humanity's special curse. But, just as she has, all through her life, intuited the simple secret of how to be happy, so, now, does she seem to feel a natural end to life's festivities without rancour or regret. I am learning not to be quite so fearful of impending death – whether it be hers or anyone else's, including my own – through her simple, peaceful, private fading away. This is her last gift of all.

Chapter Seven

One Breath Out

My brother had a lovely dog called Nutmeg, who was always the life and soul of the party. Less wary of strangers than Muffin, and certainly less territorial, he would do mad, tiny circles of delight at the first crunch of car tyre on gravel, certain that whoever was arriving would be just as ecstatic to see him as he was at their arrival. He loved a fuss. Where Muffin was always a sly sensualist, sidling up to people she liked for long, quiet, one-to-one strokes and chats, Nutmeg was a raconteur and bon viveur, positioning himself confidently in the centre of the action and making lots of happy noise. (Like owner, like dog – uncannily true, in both these cases.)

Nutmeg was a rescue dog, but he was bigger than Muffin. He had a dollop of Alsatian in his genes, but none of that breed's potential ferocity. Nutmeg was a gentle jester of a dog. He liked Muffin and she liked him, although there was the usual tussle for their respective basket space when we went to stay, and the two dogs had to be walled up at opposite ends of the house when it was time for one of them to be fed. They were each as greedy as the other, with the same disastrous results should their scavenging go undetected: copious regurgitation from one end, in the case of Nutmeg; liquid motions at the other for Muffin. Disgusting pair!

Nutmeg and Muffin were roughly the same age, so they went from playful high spirits into stiff-legged decline in a kind of parallel fading. Nutmeg also developed a wheezy cough, which caused him difficulties breathing. Towards the end of his life, he would follow my sister-in-law round the house, fixing her with a puzzled gaze, as if to say, 'Can't you do something about this? I seem to be getting old.'

Muffin's eyes have clouded over completely in the months since she turned fifteen, so the former beseeching gaze no longer haunts me. But she does wander around in my wake, from time to time, and then stand, awkwardly, in the middle of the room. The unspoken question hangs in the air: 'Who am I again, and what am I doing here – remind me?'

'Do you think she is suffering?' I ask my daughter.

'No, Mum. She's just old, that's all.'

Just old. So, in these last weeks, in what turns out to be her closing chapter, I keep the space as clean and as safe and as calm as I can for Muffin. I buy her food, give her tablets and talk to her softly. Inevitably the time approaches when thinking and writing about my dog will be forced to slip permanently from the present tense into the past.

*

The end, when it came, was just as I had always wished: gentle, calm, touched with grace. Muffin died at the end of April 2012. It was a miracle that she had made it this far, given the difficulties she faced. But there was something in her that simply would not give up. She could not leave us of her own accord. And so January came and went, then February, March and most of April. There were moments of illumination here and there: basking in the sunshine in the unusually mild March afternoons; catching an occasional riveting scent on the evening breeze by the open back door; relishing a delicious morsel from a freshly roasted chicken fed to her by hand as if she were a little pup being coaxed in the art of fine dining; or finding a comfortable resting place, somewhere quiet and warm, in which to toast her weary limbs. This was how small her world had become, but she inhabited it fully, with every ounce of her failing strength.

The hallway was now covered in plastic sheeting, for she could not make it through the night. Her incontinence was getting worse, as the arthritis continued to affect her lower back, numbing all sensation in her expulsive organs. Though it cost her dear, she always managed to heave herself from sleep and out of her basket, even if she could not make it as far as the back door or garden. One particular morning, as April drew to a close, I woke up to find her halfway down the hall, lying conked out in her own mess, and I knew the game was up. Since Muffin would never choose to wander off and die on her own, although every cell of her being now seemed to be crying out for rest, I had to make the decision for her.

Carefully, I picked her up and put her in a warm bath to make her clean and comfortable. Muffin had always loathed having a bath, and used to struggle furiously to escape, shaking angry soap bubbles over the entire house in protest at the indignity of it all, but today she let me soak her and surrendered completely to my arms as I carried her back downstairs, swaddled in towels, with just her fluffy duck's head peeking out. The sensation of the water, and the careful drying and brushing, seemed to soothe her. She curled up in her basket and fell asleep.

Then I made two calls: one to a friend whose judgement in these matters I trusted entirely and the other to Muffin's vet. When I said what had happened, the vet did not demur – all the signs were there. The dear dog had finally had enough. Most of the time on this, her last day, she just slept. There was none of the restless wandering that had been such a feature of the previous few weeks.

'I think she knows, Mum,' said my daughter, who was back from university for some time off. She was able to take a few moments alone with the dog to say her own goodbye. If Muffin did know her moment had come, then the knowledge gave her only peace. She seemed genuinely relaxed, some great weight fallen from her shoulders.

Later in the morning, as I was ringing for advice, she got out of her basket and tottered into the back room to find me. Rather than make her go back, I placed her duvet beside the sofa, folded twice for extra softness, and carefully lay the dog down on her side, since she found it difficult to make this manoeuvre on her own. Then I lay down on the sofa myself. We stayed there together for what seemed like hours, but the day was such a strange one that time was playing tricks. Sometimes I tried to sit and meditate – a posture and procedure that the dog knew well, and which had always soothed her in the past – but mostly we just lay and breathed together, each in our parallel universe, enigmatic as distant planets, but somehow in tune, connected. I slipped out for half an hour to fetch sedatives from the vet to keep her calm for his arrival. When I got back, she was in exactly the same place. She had not stirred.

The morning slid into afternoon. At three o'clock a duty vet and his assistant knocked on the door. When they came into the back room, Muffin still did not move. I am not sure she even knew they were there, which is how I wanted it. I sat by her head, stroking her ears and murmuring reassurance, while the vet clipped the thick fur on her back leg and looked for a deep vein to inject into. There was no struggle, no consternation, no fuss, no unnecessary talk. Just once, before the needle made contact, Muffin roused herself and gathered a big, shuddering breath, the way she had done right through her life when resting, as if to say, 'Hold on, isn't there something I am meant to be doing, some final duty to perform?' But I soothed and stroked her and she settled back down gratefully. The injection went in cleanly, skilfully, without pain or protest. And it was done. In a second or two, her eyes quietly closed and she drifted away. There was the hint of a smile on her face, a softness in her limbs, her body still curled up comfortably on her side in her own bed. At that moment I could not be sorry for what had been done, because it was the right thing. She was free.

The vet's assistant, who was gentle and kind throughout, brought out a little white blanket to wrap and carry Muffin in, but I had other ideas, and a blanket of my own, vivid red, to lay around her. From the countless collars and leads she had worn to the dashing bandanas we knotted jauntily at her throat, red was always Muffin's colour – the colour of passion and love, the sign of a big, big heart. I carried her out of the door myself, down the drive to the waiting car. She felt light and relaxed now in my arms, unlike the heavy awkwardness of her final weeks. Just like a young sleeping puppy, a feathery presence, yielding to a last embrace. Then I handed her over and walked back inside on my own, knowing that this was something I never wanted to do, ever, in my life again.

There is an extraordinary hush that falls on the world when someone has died. I had felt it many times before, in the bleakest of hospital wards or the most elegant of en suite hospice rooms. Everything stops, and into the empty space, like an enormous helium balloon, floating through the bluest sky, comes resolution, a deep sweet stillness. Since I am not a conventionally religious person, and have no notion of God or heaven with which to comfort myself or form some rationale,

I find it hard to explain what this is about. But there is something charged in the atmosphere – almost a molecular change – as one energy, that of the living, breathing body, gets exchanged for something else, something invisible, diffuse, ineffable. It does not last. The energy, whatever it is, moves on, and the feeling fades.

When I visited my husband Tim, within twenty minutes of him dying, I could still sense his presence powerfully in the room, as if he were hovering, peacefully enough, around his own dead body, but when I saw my mother in the mortuary, a couple of days after her death, it was too late. She was completely gone, and the sight of her body seemed almost insulting, so far removed was it from the living, laughing, utterly vital person she had been.

A friend spoke to me recently about witnessing the aftermath of a motorbike crash. The victim, a young man, was dead at the scene, and friends and neighbours were already gathered, in shock, at his side. Although the level of noise and chaos was high, with ambulance sirens wailing and people vocalising their distress, what struck my friend most was the underlying atmosphere, the sublime subtext of meaning that accompanies any exit from the world, whether gradual or sudden, planned or unexpected. 'It almost felt like a privilege to be there,' he said, although he was only a passer-by on his unsuspecting way to the shops. 'I had to walk round the corner, find somewhere out of view, and just sit quietly for a while to take it all in.' When Muffin died, I felt exactly the same thing: privileged to be a witness, awestruck at the process, and able – in an almost tangible sense – to touch the essence of her, everywhere in the room where she lay, even though Muffin, the living dog, was gone.

At every stage of development, from young dog to old, Muffin taught me something new: valuable, precious lessons in the generosity of living. All the way through, Muffin's affection and connection to me never, ever faltered: when every fibre of my being wanted to withdraw, she drew me out, again and again and again. This was a dog who had suffered nothing but neglect and abuse in the formative years of her young life, yet she was radiant in her ability simply to love. And I was grateful, finally, for this: that I could be present at the moment of her death. We saw it all through, together.

From my mid-thirties onwards, for the past twenty years, I have been involved with a sequence of serious illnesses and the deaths of those very close to me, from my best friend to my mother, my father and my husband. With all these beloved people – and others, too, in a wide circle of friends – I was present in their last days, even hours, but never once at the point of death. Every one of them slipped away while I wasn't there. It has been a source of regret, but the pattern has been consistent, up till now: all of them slipping through my fingers with bewildering speed. I think I might be inclined to do the same, when my time comes – just disappear quietly, while no one is looking.

It does leave a queasy feeling for the survivor, however, and the great mystery is no closer to being solved. How on earth does one do it? How do we die? It took my little dog to show me the way. She slipped away from the world with such simplicity and ease that I felt, as I saw it happen, the lifting of a dark taboo. True, she needed help to die, but she accepted that help with a certain gratitude, even relief. The curl of her dying lip into a smile was no rigor mortis. She left in a tiny sun's ray of satisfaction. As I watched, all the fear and oppression that had gathered in me down the years, as I watched so many people struggling to die, was suddenly erased.

I had always disbelieved the medical staff who tried so hard to reassure me that 'it was very peaceful' when the person I loved had actually died, since much that I had seen in the days leading up to that death would suggest otherwise. The dying process can indeed be apocalyptic for some, though by no means for all, but what about the moment of death itself? If Muffin's example was anything to go by, then death is no torture, no tragedy even, just a simple release: you're alive, then dead; there's nothing whatsoever to be afraid of. It's the completion of a little world.

The one person I would most like to resemble, as I grow older, is my grandmother. She had none of the advantages given to me in terms of education, training and lifestyle. Like Muffin, she had a horrible start in life. After losing her mother early, she was turned out of her home to live with a cruel aunt, who made her scrub floors and kept her away from school to work as an unpaid maid. Grandmother Elizabeth survived it all, and grew into a mellow and generous woman, who was a fine cook, with a beautiful singing voice and a naughty little chuckling laugh. She lived well into her nineties and spent the last years of her life being looked after by her daughter Ella.

One day, as she sat on the sofa and watched her daughter play cards with a friend, she said, in a quiet voice, 'Well, all I have to do now is die.' Startled, Ella asked her to repeat what she thought she had heard. Grandma just shook her head and was silent. A little while later, coming back from the kitchen with afternoon tea, Ella looked across at her mother, and saw her eyes closed, her hands folded in her lap. True to her word, she had died. If there is an art to dying, that surrender to ultimate change – and I think there probably is – then Grandmother Elizabeth certainly knew it. Muffin knew it too. They would have liked each other enormously.

There was nothing about my dog that was exceptional, really. She was just a common-or-garden mongrel with a humorous and loving disposition. When I read accounts from the Dogs Trust of creatures like Holly, a nine-year-old Labrador who recently retired after seven and a half years as a search and rescue dog – when she helped locate and save twenty-one people after the 2005 Pakistan earthquake – and think of Muffin and her rather domestic little existence, then the comparison hardly measures up. But that was the wonder of Muffin: she was a supremely ordinary little mutt.

The minute the vet drove away with the dog's body in the

back, I turned my attention to letting the world know she had died. It was then I realised just how many people's lives she had touched, 'ordinary' or not. The messages poured in from all over the country to mourn the passing of one small mongrel, or, as a friend put it, 'a very special soul'.

It is easy to sink into lethargy and deep sadness when a death has occurred, forgetting all the beauty of the life that has just finished. Muffin's final months had been arduous – for her and for us. My daughter had been anxious about Muffin for a while, not knowing what she might find when she woke in the morning or came home after being out during the day. My fear was always lurking too, together with the physical strain of lifting and manoeuvring Muffin, as her mobility was increasingly restricted. These images and experiences clouded our vision. The sweetness of the dog was temporarily lost. But other people soon reminded us.

A friend wrote from London: 'We've been talking about Muffin and what a charming and delightful dog she was. The perfect companion – engaged and interested but also happy to do her own thing quietly and contentedly. She had such a peaceful and good-natured air, combined with an unassuming comedic aspect.' And Muffin's holiday carer, Catherine, sent a helpful reminder of 'such a wonderful girl. In fact, my favourite dog by far! I have visions of her charging around the park in her red bandana . . . And that wasn't so long ago.'

Slowly, as time passes, images of the dog in her prime will undoubtedly crowd back in to replace the sad and more ponderous memories of the old dog nearing her end. In the meantime, it is gratifying to know what an influence she had, not just on her immediate family, but on a wide circle of people, whose lives she touched and influenced in some small way with her particular canine character, her natural *joie de vivre*.

'Would you like us to dispose of the body for you?' inquired the vet, after Muffin had died, and they were lifting her into the boot of their car. No, I would not. I asked for cremation instead, and the return of the ashes to me. I knew exactly where they would go, as a last little tribute to my dog. Sure enough, a delivery was made, two weeks later, in a tasteful powder blue box, with an accompanying card to say that 'Your beloved pet Muffin was individually cremated on 1ˢᵗ May 2012. Please accept our heart-felt condolences for your loss.' The care with which this had been done may seem mawkish to some, but I was touched. The sense of quiet ceremony surrounding both packaging and card exceeded anything that was done for human relatives who had been cremated (memories of an ugly plastic container, carried home in a Tesco carrier bag, sprang to mind). This does raise a question about our order of priorities, animal to human, but in terms of my immediate mourning for Muffin, it was a genuine comfort.

Unlike my dog, whose reflexes and responses to any event were fast and immediate, my own tendency is one of chronic delayed reaction. Things take time to sink in. So while the world outside was clamouring to tell me of their sadness about

Muffin – and their certainty that I was terribly upset too – I felt preternaturally calm and composed. The absence I felt, if any, was the absence of struggle and worry. It was a relief not to wonder when and how the end would come for the dog – because it was already here.

This strange serenity did not last. One evening, tired and drained, I lay down on the sofa in the back room and closed my eyes, expecting sleep to come. Tears came instead, and before I knew it I was wailing like a banshee, erupting with those strange hiccuping sobs that lack any Hollywood sheen of photogenic sadness, but leave you looking swollen-eyed, snotty and blotched. In short, I was utterly and irrevocably undone. The body has its reasons, of course. I had lain in the wrong place – exactly where I sat with Muffin on her last day. But at least the poison poured out with the tears. I can sit there again peacefully now.

Grief's second wave overwhelmed me a week later and this demanded action rather than surrender. Before I knew it, I was up on my feet – cold, damp evening though it was – and off to the woods to walk it off. This was a first time on familiar paths without my dog by my side. And I realised, as I stumbled along, that what I had nervously anticipated the previous autumn – the dog walker caught wandering about on her own – was now a reality. Still, there was balance and inevitability in the action. So many had gone through this process before I had, with the wood remaining sturdy and implacable throughout.

I remembered meeting a man early one morning when

walking Muffin several years previously. It was a warm spring day, sunny and bright, but he was inconsolable, because his elderly greyhound had recently died. He wept openly and without any shame as he told me all about her: how he had walked for such a long time with her at his side and now must walk without her in her honour. I sympathised at the time, but only now do I really understand: the path *itself* simply has to be trod.

The following day I took the powder blue tube to the woods with me and scattered Muffin's ashes under the big holly tree where I had put some of Tim's ashes the year before. Man and dog together. By some peculiar coincidence, when I looked in my diary later, I saw that in the Christian calendar it was Ascension Day. I stood, as I have so many times before, with my back to the holly, looking out at the view before me. Bracken was uncurling skyward in the pale light. There was a mass of blue-bells carpeting the earth, and old steady oak trees standing tall amongst them. The recent endless rain had made everything lush and green and overgrown. When Muffin was alive and well, she found these stops for contemplation – something I was always rather fond of making – utterly incomprehensible. She always sat and waited for me, because she was a faithful hound, but there was a puzzlement in her expression, an impatience barely concealed. 'Why are we lingering so long? There's masses more to see, and a whole wood to run through. Let's get on with it.' Perhaps some memory of this was with me now, because I did not stand there for more than a moment. I had performed the last deed for my dog, and I walked on briskly, if not with a spring in my step, then at least with a sense of resolve. A contract had been honoured.

'The house must seem really empty,' someone said the other day. She has a new puppy and already cannot imagine the home without her, so much does this dog inhabit the space with her indefatigable verve and bounce. It's true: the hall has never been so tidy, the house never smelled so sweet. A whole layer of experience, movement and life has been lifted and erased, a furry mass of energy and love gone. For the first time in years I can do my yoga and back stretches without getting up from the floor with dog hair on my trousers – or in my mouth.

The real absence is more subtle than that of her physical form, and it catches me sideways at odd moments in unexpected ways. The sun has at last started to shine as spring moves into early summer. Yesterday I looked through my rear-view mirror in the car and saw the unmistakable smudges left by Muffin's nose as she gazed out of the window on one of our innumerable jaunts to here, there and everywhere. The sudden brightness of the sun not only revealed my lamentable lack of car-cleaning skills, but also showed hidden evidence of my dog, like ancient markings etched on dark cave walls, traces of another time and place. I shall never wash that window now!

On the day Muffin died, I immediately put her bedding in the bin. The sight of an empty basket was not to be borne, and it was not in a state to be handed on. We kept just one of her toys and perched it on the top of the bookcase in the hall to keep guard, but that was not the end of it, it seems. Little things keep re-emerging, small tokens of Muffin, to take me by surprise: a dusty and spotty red neckerchief shoved in a corner out of sight . . . an old ball-on-a-rope lurking under the spade behind the shed . . . a bag of dog food, unopened and bought just days before she died. None of these things makes me sad. They are just markers of her irrepressible spirit: the one who loved to eat and to show off, in her dashing bandanas; the one who pressed her nose so eagerly against the car window, waiting for the moment when she would be released, once again, to do what she always loved best, like Marilyn Monroe in *Some Like It Hot* – running wild.

There is a poem by Phoebe Hesketh about a girl called Sally. Sally, it reads, was an unstoppable force, often misunderstood and scolded by parents and teachers, and fettered by convention, when all she wanted was to be outside, ripping through the hedgerows, and burning her young skin golden in the heat. No matter how much adults tried to make her behave and simmer down, no matter the restrictions of home and school, 'they couldn't take the shine out of her./ Even when it rained/ you felt the sun saved under her skin.' When I first read this poem, I did not think it was about a girl at all, despite the evidence of my eyes. So perfectly did the spirit of Sally suit my dog, I almost felt it was written for her. Muffin, like Sally, did not always have an easy life. In many ways, she lived a life of care and of duty: to Tim, primarily, in his hard struggle with illness and incapacitation; then to Molly, during her transition from girl to adolescent, amidst the loss of her beloved father; and, finally, to me, steering me on, as she did, through widowhood, single motherhood and, last of all, guiding me into solitude and a new beginning, as my daughter negotiated the adult world and started to fly away. Muffin took much responsibility upon herself unasked. There was within her a seriousness of purpose, a dedication, not taught nor expected but freely given. Still, her natural good humour and buoyancy never deserted her, well into old age and failing health. Her spirit soared. And in that flight, we all – the ones who met and loved her – were lifted high.

I listened recently to a programme on the radio about a man called Stuart Jessop, who undertook an eight-month walk of 2,500 miles all around the United Kingdom in aid of two mental health charities. Stuart himself suffers from depression and knows not only how isolating that condition is, but also how helpful the process of physical activity – the simple act of walking – can be for mind and body. Although often the only human for miles on his epic adventure, he was never entirely alone. There was one crucial, consistent companion during his long endeavour: his springer spaniel, Poppy. Poppy, whom we heard bouncing backwards and forwards throughout the programme, constantly checking on her master with an admirable solicitude, was not only friend and helpmeet, a safeguard against loneliness and fear, but also a conduit for communication, a lightning rod of precious contact with the world. Unlikely to strike up a conversation on his own, the dog always broke down barriers.

Said Stuart, 'I've probably talked to more strangers in the last year than I've talked to in the rest of my life.' When Poppy injured herself, and had to go home for a brief recuperation, he really noticed a change. 'During those two weeks, I hardly spoke to anyone . . . There's a big difference between man on his own, walking, or dog with owner, walking. Poppy's been a tremendous help.'

In the absence of my own unique little buffer zone, Muffin, I am trying to be bold in stepping out alone. This morning I walked to the woods. It was bright and early and the sun was deliciously inviting. Although it was only half past seven, there were plenty of people already around – a few schoolchildren, dragging their feet and dawdling, some harassed workers heading for the bus, and the usual motley cohort of dog walkers, strolling along with their pets. I made a point of acknowledging everyone I passed. The ones on their own nodded briefly, keen to move on with all due speed, and slightly discomfited, in that very bashful English way, at being greeted in public by a perfect stranger. It was the ones with the dogs, even those I didn't know, who immediately engaged with me and were happy to linger for a chat. The conversation was inconsequential, but never mind. The connection – between earth and animal, animal and human – was made. What a rich and deep connection it is, that these ordinary dogs, without a second thought, provide: like a comfort blanket thrown around shivering shoulders to keep out the existential cold.

The longest conversation I had this particular morning was

with the owner of elderly Bounce and 'Puppy Dog', or Sam. Back in the old days, Muffin and Bounce would sniff and frolic a little, as they had a bit of a crush on each other, whilst the more nervous and jealous Sam would skitter off sideways, waiting to get rid of Muffin and win Bounce back all for himself. Bounce died a few months ago, and now Sam goes for walks without him. He knows me well enough, but, shy as he is, would never, up till now, come up to me, despite a friendly proferred hand and vocal encouragement, but today was different.

At first sight of me, he veered off into the bushes as usual, but then, as I stood and talked, he came closer – uninvited – and pushed his nose into my hand. I was telling his owner that Muffin had died. 'Oh, he knows,' she said, as Sam suddenly came up and stood by me, then ran off for a sniff around, only to return for a further, more lingering snuffle and stroke. But what did he know? That Muffin was dead? Impossible. Still, dogs are smart. He had never seen me in the wood on my own before. Something had happened and he had noticed it. He was emboldened, I like to think, not just by the absence of his companion and my 'rival' dog, cramping his space, but by a simple act of generosity and kindness, dog to human: I will be your friend. It helped me a lot.

Elsewhere in the wood, when the walkers had all disappeared from view, and I was alone, with the bluebells now fading and dying underfoot, and an enormous canopy forming overhead, as the trees expanded into their summer finery – their hats and bonnets and pretty green parasols giving leaf shade, colour and cool – I had the strangest and loveliest sensation. Suddenly, everywhere I went, I could feel Muffin's presence in the space around me. All trace of her old age and infirmity was gone. She was young again and running, light-footed and invisible, just a few elusive steps up ahead, her fur snagged occasionally by the brambles, and wearing, as she so often did in real life, a nonchalant leaf in her long, tangled ear. And that, for me, is where she will be now, like the puff of a dandelion's head seeded lightly in the breeze: dancing, somewhere in the undergrowth and over the bumpy dirt tracks of this simple little wood. On, on and on. Forever.

Acknowledgements

In memory of Sandy, Maggie Graham's special rescue dog, who died in summer 2012.

So many people gave time, love and shelter to my dog, it is hard to do them justice. You all know who you are, so, THANK YOU, from Muffin and from me. Special awards of merit go to Neil Stoddard at Beechwood Vets, Chapel Allerton, Leeds, for his tender loving care, and Brendan Clarke at Tower Wood Vets, Leeds, for the homeopathic touch. Several homes and families welcomed Muffin in, whenever we were away, chiefly: Roger and Rose Brady; Bridget Kelbrick; Libby and Phil Mountford; Steve and Rebecca Besford; Catherine and Joe Mellor. She loved you all! For twelve years, come rain, hail or shine, the dog walkers of Gipton Wood provided canine play-mates for Muffin – and human ones for me. And the RSPCA Leeds deserve considerable applause here – for rescuing a half-starved mongrel in the first place, and then offering her to us. What a gift.

On the literary front, I want to thank the unsung heroes of the writing world, the Royal Literary Fund, for helping me financially when times were hard; Melissa Benn, for *always* inspiring me onwards, as a writer and as a friend; and Jane Turnbull, whose whole idea this was in the first place, and whom I am proud to have as an agent, a pal, and a peerless mentor. For his uncanny ability to capture my dog's soul on camera, I salute Johnny Ring, and, for her delicacy of doggy design, Liane Payne. Finally, great gratitude goes to editors Kerri Sharp and Briony Gowlett at Simon & Schuster, for having faith in the story – and in the little dog herself. She will live forever now.

About the Author

Barney Bardsley is an author and freelance journalist who lives in Leeds with her daughter Molly. She writes features for the *Guardian*, *Psychologies* Magazine, *Woman's Weekly*, *Yorkshire Post* and *Femail*. When not writing she gardens, sings with an unruly choir called Good in Parts, and is trying – against all the odds – to learn Hungarian.